The ABC's

of Dog Training

...and You!

HOW TO TRAIN YOUR DOG –
THE TRUTH, THE WHOLE TRUTH
AND NOTHING BUT... THE TRUTH!

by David Ruiz

Instructor of Blind Persons and Guide Dogs
Director – A Better Canine School for Dogs
San Diego, California

THE ABC'S OF DOG TRAINING...AND YOU!
How To Train Your Dog, The Truth, The Whole Truth,
And Nothing But... The Truth!
By David Ruiz

Published By:

 David Ruiz, ABC (A Better Canine) School for Dogs
7330 University Avenue
La Mesa, CA 91941-6003

Library of Congress Cataloging-in-Publication Data
Ruiz, David / ABC (A Better Canine) School for Dogs
The ABC's of Dog Training...and You!
How To Train Your Dog, The Truth, The Whole Truth,
And Nothing But... The Truth! By David Ruiz.

ISBN 0 9663125-0-3
$24.95 Softcover

The ABC's

of Dog Training

...and You!

BY DAVID RUIZ

A BASIC OBEDIENCE AND BEHAVIOR COURSE

THIS BOOK IS YOUR CONSTANT REFERENCE, THE FIRST AND THE LAST WORD IN THE RECOGNITION, THE TRAINING, THE UNDERSTANDING, AND THE MAKING OF YOU AND YOUR DOG - THE BEST OF FRIENDS! YOU WILL LOVE IT!

GRADUATES

School for Dogs

SAN DIEGO

DEDICATION

In Love and Memory

of

The Dog

All our furry, wonderful, lifetime companions

Yours and Mine

Past ... Present ... Future

We remember and are thankful!

For your love!
For your kisses!
For your antics!
For your willfulness!
For your warmth!

As your name – **DOG** – suggests when spelled backwards,

As HE "watches" over all our loved ones we know

He "watches" over you!

ACKNOWLEDGMENTS

"Prince"
(On front cover)
The inspiration behind this book!
May God bless him – always!

Diana Dean
My partner, friend, secretary and assistant, whose
loyalty and constant endeavor immensely
contributed to the writing of this book.

Stanley Doran and Walter Doran, Founders
Pilot Dogs, Inc.
A school for the training of guide dogs
and their blind masters.

Clark Kelly, D.V.M.
For his friendship, encouragement
and contributions.

Berit Jacobson-Kinter
For her friendship, devotion, encouragement
and production expertise.

Self-Publishing Partners, San Diego, California
Larry, Jeanne and Darryl DiRuscio, Ken and Debbi
Seaney. For their cover design, support and
contributions.
May God bless them...all!

J.M.J.

In honor and loving memory of

Angel Ruiz and Aida Ruiz

My Father "Papa" and My Mother "Mama"

and

My Lifetime Companions

Titana, Rusty I, Rusty II, Rusty III, Sammy, Honey,
Rambo, Champ, Prince, Winston and Romeo

Blessed...you are!

TABLE OF CONTENTS

Success Stories 3

To The Reader
   The Why Behind This Book 17

Introduction To Successful Training 25

A Through Z Dog Names 33

Lesson 001: Housebreaking and Managing
   Your Puppy... or Older Dog 51

Lesson 101: A Through Z — Tid-Bits to
   Ponder and Remember 83

Lesson 102: The Psychology of Training 105

Lesson 103: Basic Equipment 149

Lesson 104: The Heel Command —
   Beginning Techniques 167

Lesson 105: The Heel Command —
   Advanced Techniques 181

Lesson 106: The Sit and Stay Command 207

Lesson 107: Solving Misbehavior Situations 223

Lesson 108: The Down and Stay Command 267

Lesson 109: The Come Command 289

THE ADVANCED LESSONS
SERIES 200

Lesson 201: The Unsupervised Stay Command

Master Out-of-Sight......................................307

Lesson 202: The Go To Your Place or

Outside Command 315

Lesson 203: Automobile Riding Techniques

You Don't Deserve a "Wrrrruf" Ride from

Your Dog! 323

Lesson 204: The Halt Command 339

Lesson 205: Boundary Limit Techniques 345

Lesson 206: A Final... Extremely Important

Thought...To Ponder! 353

Summary of Lessons and Off-Leash Control 363

Graduation 377

Postscript 391

Post Postscript 393

Certificate of Completion 395

A WORD OF CAUTION
DISCLAIMER

The majority of "dog" problems ARE NOT dog problems ... !

Happiness is... **A Better Canine!**

SUCCESS STORIES FROM GRADUATES AND VETERINARIANS

It has always been my opinion that before **success** to an endeavor **can** be attained, one **must have** confidence and trust in oneself and the lesson plan.

The **basis** of this book is **confidence – for you – the leader of the pack;** for if your dog views **you** in this manner, success can't help but be yours!

At ABC School for Dogs, **before** a student signs up for our program, we invite them to the school, where we show them our credentials.

The most reliable source of reference that we have found is word-of-mouth from graduates and professionals that have experienced **the fruits** of our successful methods!

For your information and evaluation, a sampling of our references follow.

Sincerely,
ABC (A Better Canine) School for Dogs

David Ruiz, Director

May 29, 1990

Dear David,

I want to thank you on behalf of McDuff, and myself for the comprehensive training sessions that brought McDuff from a very independent and strong willed terrier, to an obedient little gentleman, without breaking his spirit or changing his personality.

Each session was a challenge, but learning and practicing your instructions, they were challenges easily met.

I also want to tell you again how thankful I am that you instructed me on how to fend off an attacking dog. As I told you, we were walking along when a dog ran accross his yard and over a board fence and came charging us. With my heart in my mouth, I remembered what you said to do I unleashed MCDuff, picked him up and started to swing his leash in a circular motion, and the dog did not try to go past the leash. It stopped him !!! Mc Duff and I walked slowly away with me still swinging the leash. The dog followed, barking, for a few feet and then stopped.

Thank you again, because truthfully, McDuff is A Better Canine !!!!

Sincerely,

Georgett Middleton
3009 Plaza Leonardo
Bonita, CA 92002

P.S. You have my persission to use McDuffs picture for your book, or any P.R.,also you have my permission to use any part or all of my letter.

Stoorza Ziegaus & Metzger

October 7, 1998

Mr. David Ruiz
7330 University Avenue
La Mesa, CA 91941

Dear David,

Watching you train Morley, our wonderful Golden Retriever, was like watching Picasso paint, or Nureyev dance...or Bill Gates using Windows. You're not only a master of your trade, you're clearly the master of the dog--which is what you try to teach owners to be.

My family and I were enthralled as we listened to your very personal "lectures." You're also a natural-born public speaker!

You've been a very important part of our lives in that your wonderful training of Morley led to a 12-year love affair between us and the marvelous four-legged member of our family. As soon as our grieving subsides, we'll be calling upon you to start the process again.

Thank you for allowing me to read the draft of your book. It put me right back into the training session with you and Morley. Now every dog owner in the world will have the benefit...and the privilege...of having as wonderful a relationship with their dog as we had as a result of our David Ruiz training!

Fondly,

Gail Stoorza-Gill
Chairman & CEO
Stoorza, Ziegaus & Metzger, Inc.

August 31, 1990

We recently completed David Ruiz's course in obedience training
with our Corgi, Bentley. We found that his step-by-step drills
and exercises changed our dog's behavior immensely. Even after
the first meeting we noticed an immediate improvement. It trans-
formed Bentley from an exuberant and uncontrollable animal into
quite a well-behaved gentleman who now respects us and responds
to our commands. We are indebted to David for this.

We found David Ruiz to be very friendly and extremely knowledgable
about dog behavior and we appreciated his thorough explanations.
His training program was formulated with a great deal of thought
and planning. David was enthusiastic and dedicated to his teaching. His demonstrations were clear and concise and, more importantly, worked like he said they would! We are so happy with the
results and recommend him heartily.

Pam Adair

Jerry Petrone

September 10, 1987

Dear David,

   Here,s the picture of " the graduate" we promised. Brandon
may have learned "sit", "heel", and "stay", but he hasn't quite
learned to smile.

   Both John and I want to thank you for the transformation of
our " hard head". Brandon has changed from a wild animal to a
loveable, obedient (most of the time) pet. When we brought him
in the first time, I was sure that nobody would be able to
control that dog. Boy, was I wrong!

   It was hard work training Brandon, and still is, but it very
rewarding. I'm convinced that a trained dog is a happy dog and
that owners of well trained dogs enjoy their pets 100%.

                    Sincerley, two satisified customers,

                    Donna Jones

                    John Jones

                    Donna Jones &

                    John Jones

BOULEVARD ANIMAL CLINIC
CLARK KELLY, D.V.M.
7047 El Cajon Boulevard
San Deigo, CA 92115
(619) 582-7250

David Ruiz
ABC School for Dogs
P.O. Box 37
La Mesa, CA 92044

Dear David:

It doesn't seem like it has been 11 years since your dog, "Prince,"
on command, jumped up on the examination table. I was amazed at
him performing this act. I had never seen an animal perform this
difficult maneuver.

Through your training methods, animal behavior has been improved
and a stronger human/animal bond can exist. We have so often
seen where a trained dog became, not only "A Better Canine," but
also, a better patient; certainly, a lot easier to treat. Many
companion animals and their families will have a longer and better
relationship in life.

I congratulate you on your book and wish you success in the future.

Sincerely,

Clark Kelly, D.V.M.

CK/rae

P.S. You have my permission to publish this letter in whole or
in part.

PALM RIDGE PET CLINIC
4370 PALM AVE.
SAN DIEGO, CALIFORNIA 92154

July 22, 1990

    As a veterinarian and a student of David Ruiz, I strongly recommend obedience training for all dogs, not just the large breeds. Behavioral problems are the most common reasons dogs are euthanised and this could be easily resolved with the proper training.

    I refer many of my clients to David and they have all been completely satisfied with the teaching methods and their "new dog". There are other obedience trainers in San Diego and I see many graduates of these other schools, but I believe David uses the best methods and his graduates are much easier to treat as patients.

    I was very satisfied with the training I received with my Saint Bernard "Bacardi" and am now in training with my new Saint Bernard puppy, "Kahlua".

Jo Beaty, DVM
Jo Beaty, DVM

I give permission to David Ruiz to use my letter and picture of Kahlua in his new obedience book.

HOME FEDERAL

Bill N. Kinter
First Vice President
Chief Marketing Officer

"0" Broadway, Suite 1200
San Diego, California 92101
(619) 699-8322

July 5, 1990

Dear David,

To think that we almost gave away our loveable and beautiful Golden Retriever, Autumn. From 8 weeks old to 1½ years she wreaked havoc on our lives. We referred to her as "the wild woman". Then our veterinarian referred us to you.

Even after the very first lesson, she began to change into the wonderful companion that she is today. She's part of the family even to the point of greeting guests like a lady (admittedly an occasional lapse where sheer excitement brings out a happy jump). She then remains part of the festivities and not the center of them. Walks in Balboa Park both on and off the leash is probably her most favorite activity.

Thank-you David for turning our "wild woman" into a gentlewoman.

Sincerely,

Bill & Berit Kinter

Bill & Berit Kinter

Lou Ann Lester
John Reighley
4870 Harbinson Avenue
La Mesa, CA 91941

Dear David,

We can't say enough about your school. Since attending your classes,
CHARMIN has been wonderful. Using your simple techniques has
changed CHARMIN from a beast into a well-behaved dog that we have
always wanted. We take pleasure in having CHARMIN accompanying
us on our outings now. People are always saying how well behaved
she is. Your help was greatly appreciated and we are looking forward
to taking the advanced classes.

Thank You,

John & Lou Ann & Charmin.

**DAVID WITH TWO OF HIS BEST CANINES
PRINCE AND HONEY**

ABOUT THE AUTHOR

Mr. Ruiz was born in Guatemala, located in Central America. In January 1955, when he was 12 years old, he immigrated to the United States. Soon after, he became associated with Pilot Dogs, Inc., a school for the training of guide dogs for the blind. There he served as kennel-boy, interpreter for Spanish-speaking blind students, trainer, and instructor.

He attended Ohio State and Franklin Universities in Columbus, Ohio, and during the Viet Nam era, served in the United States Marine Corps. Since 1979, he has been the Owner/Director of ABC (A Better Canine) School for Dogs in San Diego, California.

Mr. Ruiz is a very quiet and gentle person; otherwise, humorous, strong and commanding! When asked his wishes regarding this page: "People don't want to hear about me; they want to know how to properly walk their dog, how to keep him from barking while they're away from home, and how to keep him from being a juvenile delinquent. They really want to know about...THE LEADER OF THE PACK!"

When asked, "Who is the leader in your pack?" without hesitating, with a wink and slight grimace, his answer, "Prince... of course!"

DAVID AND HONEY

DAVID AND WINSTON

**LEFT TO RIGHT
RAMBO, SIMONE (A GUEST), CHAMP (BARELY
VISIBLE BEHIND DAVID), WINSTON (BEHIND FENCE),
AND HONEY**

TO THE READER
THE WHY BEHIND THIS BOOK

This book is on **basic** dog training and nothing else but **basic** dog training! Its purpose is not to cause your dog to become a Rin Tin Tin, Lady, or a Tramp, but simply a **better** family (pack) member, and a **better** citizen of the community – overall, **"A Better Canine."**

Why should a lifetime of 13 to 18 years that you spend with your dog be traumatic, when it can be happy! Picture Mary in Poway, California, and her 8-month-old Dalmatian, Beatrice, who told me, "She likes to jump on people under 6 and over 60!" Then there's Kathy in Jamul, and her Yorkshire Terrier, Bullet, "...who wants to charge every dog in sight, and when we get home he goes ballistic!" Kathy's dog may be a Yorkshire Terrier, but his ego is as big as any Rottweiler; plus the name that she's given him doesn't help either. This "Rottweiler Syndrome" in many cases also applies to Chihuahuas, Cairn Terri-

ers, Cocker Spaniels, Dachshunds, Bichon Frise and
other small dog breeds. Last, but not least, we have
Tarzan in La Jolla, one of the most notorious Beagles
that I have ever seen – he **eats** Toyotas and spits out
jalopies! This Tarzan actually ate and destroyed the
interior of his owner's classic Mercedes Benz con-
vertible. To avoid these scenarios, let's take a serious
look at basic dog training.

By **basic** dog training, we mean teaching your dog
a conduct that will provide both of you with a **har-
monious** life together. Though some of the lessons
taught in this book are considered advanced: the Stay
Command – With You Out-of-Sight and the Boundary Limit Techniques, we consider them **basic** lessons that **all** dogs should know, and that will help
you reach your goals.

If you wish to know about picking the right puppy,
nutrition, medicine, grooming, boarding, or breed-
ing, we suggest that you seek the correct and corresponding source. Our goal with this book is to **teach
you** how to train your dog to be a compatible family
(pack) member, and to do so in a manner to avoid
rummaging through countless pages and useless
words that can cloud the issues and/or play on the
unsuspecting sentimentality of human emotions.

My experience regarding many of the books written and many of the obedience classes offered is that due to a sort of "code of silence" in dog training circles, the trend has been NOT TO TELL THE WHOLE TRUTH! The issue of training is always "soft pedaled!" The reason for this, I believe, is fear that owners may not understand "real" training methods, and therefore, may be offended.

Precedence is always given to the perceived sentimentality of the human. I believe that this patronizing point of view underestimates the intelligence of dog owners. I first began to discover these situations when, at the age of fifteen, my thirst and search for the subject was to no avail! It was at this time that I became involved in training guide dogs for the blind and instructing blind persons in the use of their guide dogs. During my many years of training guide dogs and as Director of A Better Canine School for Dogs in San Diego, California, my findings have always provided the following contradictions and the lack of true facts:

"That...there are NO BAD DOGS!"

"That...the dog LIVES to please you!"

"That...THE ONLY WAY to train a dog is through love!"

"That...THE ONLY WAY to train a dog is by rewarding him with a cookie!"

"That...you CAN NOT correct the dog unless
you catch him in the act."
"That...you CAN NEVER use your hand on the
dog."
"That...the dog SHOULD NEVER cower to the
owner."
"That...the dog HAS a short memory."

How many headaches, expenses, and dogs' lives
could have been saved if we stuck with the truth and
not listened **and believed** that, "You can't teach an
old dog new tricks." Once again, I am here to tell you
that that is **pure bunk.** The truth of it is, that basically a dog — barring extremes — **can...learn...at...
any...age!**

Many incorrect methods have grown and many
old wives' tales exist. In group classes the rote method
is always taught. Dog owners never know the **why**
behind the **"Push there and pull here!"** and the **"Pull
here and push there!"** and so on. Due to this di-
lemma, most relationships between the human and
the dog **never mature** to their full potential.

The lessons in this book are written in a step-by-
step method, giving the reader understanding and
background of the **why** behind the various steps. In

the interest of candor, a ghost writer/editor has not been employed. The lessons are written in precisely the manner in which they are given at ABC (A Better Canine) School for Dogs, and the lessons are **only** concerned with this subject matter:

THE TRAINING OF YOU AND YOUR DOG.

At ABC School for Dogs we have found that owners can, **in fact**, easily handle the truth. They **enthusiastically** embrace the professional methods we employ and are amazed at the results. Their reward is that they are able to realize the full potential of the relationship between themselves and their dog.

For years I have been an ardent follower of Dale Carnegie's teachings on human relations. For more than fifty years thousands, if not millions, of people have succeeded in bettering their lives through Carnegie's human relation practices. When I set out to write this book, my hope was that, as is the case with Dale Carnegie disciples, the readers of **this** book would **never again** have to resort to any other text in the training, the understanding, the loving and the development of the kind of Master/Dog relations that **truly** make for each other **"The Best of Friends!"**

The human should no longer have to **learn to**

live with an unruly dog that literally dominates the household. To accomplish the task at hand, it is suggested that you not only read the contents of this book from cover to cover but chew it, savor it and digest it. The results to be derived by you and your dog will be...**unparalleled**. Throughout this book, the **KISS** principle applies. Without meaning to offend anyone's intelligence, we use the coined phrase only for emphasis of its valuable intent: **"Keep It Simple Stupid"..."Keep It Short and Simple."**

Hence:

THE ABC'S OF DOG TRAINING...AND YOU! THE TRUTH, THE WHOLE TRUTH, AND NOTHING BUT...THE TRUTH!

"WELCOME!"

ROMEO

Meet my 14-month-old, Romeo, who, "totally out of control" came into my family only a few months ago. Though beautiful and a real lover, I am not totally convinced as to his "smarts." Romeo believes the whole of life is only ... "a ball!" When I first brought him home, we stopped to have a hamburger and Romeo dropped part of his behind the truck driver's seat; and, don't you know, that though months have gone by, each and every time we have gotten into the truck since, the first thing he does is to go look for that piece of hamburger. Romeo just might prove to be my ... "dunce!" That silly puppy! But, gosh ... do I ever love him!

PAULA FALLS AND RIPPER

INTRODUCTION TO
SUCCESSFUL TRAINING

Because training dogs entails many variables, no one can guarantee results which are always positive. Success is highly dependent on the response ability of the dog and the master, the temperament of both, follow-through of training methods and training on a daily basis. Our experience at ABC (A Better Canine) School for Dogs has been that if the key elements are conscientiously applied, success to the basics of training can be readily attained.

But the basics of training are more than just **basic**! It is through their application that you will learn to control your dog at all times. When you visit the veterinarian, you'll no longer need to call on the United States Marine Corps or the National Guard to keep your dog under control and your vet's office in one piece. Through **the basics** your dog learns that **YOU** are the master/leader of the pack, not he. Should he have a tendency to be aggressive, obedience training is the first step in controlling him.

Different dog trainers will give you different opinions in the training of your dog. Our methods are designed for the master/dog team. We firmly believe that they **can not** be separated. This isn't my original idea, and credit must be given where credit is due. The basis for it comes from my many years of association—as kennel-boy, interpreter, trainer, and instructor—with Pilot Dogs, Inc., 625 West Town Street, Columbus, Ohio 43215, a school for training guide dogs and their blind masters; and with Stanley and Walter Doran who are the originators and founders, and Wayne Mathys, their Director of Training.

There are no magic tricks. If you have the time and patience, you can train your own dog. **Time and patience** are of the utmost importance, as are **affection, discipline, love, and clear directions.**

To encourage you to slow down, **bold** type is used throughout the book. It is also used for emphasis and clarity of major points and to teach **you,** as we do with the students at our school, the manner in which our communication should be perceived by our dogs: not necessarily loud, but **clear, firm, sharp and to-the-point!**

Before you begin any "official" training—especially if you obtain an older dog—it's preferable to develop a strong and loving bond between you and your dog. Wait at least two to three weeks. The stronger the bond, the more responsive your dog will be to your training. A supply of lifelong **toys** will enhance the relationship.

Be it a small or a large dog, a guide dog for the blind, a hearing dog, a police dog, or your own dog, they **all** learn obedience and behavior by the very same methods.

Formal training should not commence until your dog is **approximately** 6-months-old. Some **may** and some **should** start earlier, especially if your dog is of the giant type, but no earlier than 4 months. Until this time the dog hasn't developed sufficient mature patterns. He lives in a Disneyworld of all fun and games. During this time the emphasis should be socialization, **informal** training, and the development of his personality. **Formal** training prior to the correct age could be a traumatic experience not only for your dog, but for you as well. You will know that the time is right when you begin to wonder, "Just who owns who anyhow?" and begin feeling that the home you live in is no longer yours!

The difference between **informal and formal training** is that in formal training definite discipline enters into the picture. With informal training, discipline is applied only in a very light manner, and only to housebreaking behaviors. We must remember that the puppy is, after all, **a puppy**!

DISCIPLINE

Would you as a parent abuse your child? Of course not. Then do not abuse your dog! Discipline should be stern, but **never** heavy-handed. **Extreme judgement** must be used—judgement that depends on temperament, size, strength and weight of your dog. In addition, once the correction is understood, **it's over!** You must now forget it and go back to love. But remember...when corrections are required, they should be **swift and stern.** It's better to correctly correct once, than to have to correct for a lifetime!

In training your dog, expose him to the maneuver or behavior that's desired, and through love and affection encourage him to perform. This requires repetition and, in some cases, much patience – patience which can not be lost! To lose your patience could cause your dog to lose his spirit, a not too pleasant experience for your dog...a not too pleasant experience for you!

Dogs do not learn by osmosis; **there are no two ways about it, you have to practice with them. Practice does make perfect!** There is nothing more irritating to the instructor, and unfair and unkind to the dog, than students who arrive at the school 5 minutes prior to class to "practice" what was taught in the previous session. As a building can not stand without its foundation, neither can the training of your dog.

Once your dog learns the maneuvers and commands being taught and subsequently disobeys, **then** you can take corrective actions, but not until you are sure that **he does** understand. You can correct your dog of unfavorable behavior patterns by taking corrective action **immediately** when the undesired behavior occurs. Follow through by **negatively** (negative reinforcement is defined in Lesson 107) encouraging him to display the undesired behavior. At the same time use **clear and firm** corrective remarks, i.e., "NO, FIDO. YOU DON'T DO THAT! YOU ARE A BAD BOY!"

A romp after each training session is relaxing for both members of the team and will extremely aid in the training process.

The **occasional** dog treat (goodies) is also very good; however, this **should not** become the rule for every time that the dog performs. In other words, do not be like so many people with their dogs who train them the "cookie way" and say to the dog, "sit" and "cookie"; "sit" and "cookie"; "sit" and "cookie" for the day **will come** when you won't have a cookie. Then you'll get no sit. On the other hand, a treat must be given each and every time he does perform. The treat – a simple pat on the head and/or encouraging remarks, "Good boy, good boy!"

In response to more advanced commands, such as the Come Command, there should be more emphasis on showing your approval. Your treat for him, as Dale Carnegie proposes, "Be hearty in your approbation, and lavish in your praise." **As with people, you will be amazed at how eager your dog will be to repeat the performance.**

Before you expect your dog to respond to more advanced training commands, he should, without question, first understand that **YOU, in fact, are the LEADER.** He should also understand and be able to respond to the basic commands without hesitation or fault. **The basic commands to be taught are:**

- No!
- Heel
- Sit and Stay
- Down and Stay
- Sit from the Down
- Go to Your Place / Go Outside
- Come
- Tone Command – "Ahhh!" or "Uhuh!" Such as in, "Don't you dare do that! Uhuh!" (or Ahhh!)

You'll find that if you use this tone, in a very commanding way, you will immediately get your dog's attention...and stop him in his tracks to – whatever!

But training does not begin with your dog; it begins with **YOU**! You must first have a general understanding of:

A. What you want to accomplish.

B. The proper use of the training equipment.

C. The nature of how a dog actually learns. We refer to this as the psychology of the dog...and...on this note...training begins.

But first, **essential for you** is Lesson 101, A Through Z Tid-Bits To Ponder and Remember! Also, if your dog is a puppy, Lesson 001, Housebreaking and Managing Your Puppy; but, better yet, no matter what your position, READ THIS ENTIRE BOOK FROM COVER TO COVER — there is a "filet mignon" to be had in each and every section. TREAT YOURSELF!

KIMBERLY AND JIMMY
RAIN, DAKOTA AND LACY

"The kids no longer have 'accidents.' What a difference training has made! They are super dogs. God bless you always."

A THROUGH Z DOG NAMES

Joey and Jennifer were insistent that their pet turtle, Tommy, should have a frog companion. The story goes that to fulfill their wishes, Jeff and Debbie, in spite of night drawing near, agreed to make a dash with them to the neighborhood pond. They didn't name the little frog when they returned because it was dark, late and bedtime. It was a sad morning for tearful Joey and Jennifer when they found that Tommy Turtle had during the night eaten the little frog, "Before we even named him!" So, posthumously they agreed that the little frog's name would be "Hop-a-long-casualty." A name perfectly suited for an ingested little frog – but not for a dog.

Which brings us to the name that we give our pet – the dog. This name has three elements:

A. The **actual** name that we choose.

B. The **effect** that the name may have on the personality/temperament of the dog.

C. The **sound** that is heard by the dog.

So often we have had students that **puzzle** and **ponder** as to just what name do we give our dog? We have named him DOGGIE, but only on a temporary basis. We have looked in the library and at pet stores for lists of dog names...to no avail. To aid you in this process, following are names that have been used by our students for their dogs. **We do not necessarily recommend all of them.**

When choosing your dog's name we recommend to stay away from names that could easily affect the dog's personality and temperament. Avoid names that would negatively and/or positively play on material properties or human actions, such as: Killer, Ripper, Rocky, Sugar, Sweetpea, or Chrysanthemum...unless of course, you in fact want the affect of those properties.

Living in San Diego, California we receive many calls from Mexican Spanish speaking residents wanting to know if we can train their dog using Spanish commands. I explain that we would be glad to, however, we don't encourage it because commands, as the name that we give our dog , should be short, one or two syllables and clear in tone when said. A tone that should **capture** the dog's attention and be easily discerned by him; otherwise, picture: "SIEN-TA-TE!" vs. "SIT!" and "PRIN-CI-PE!" vs. "PRINCE!"

That... "you CANNOT change a dog's name," is just one more of the UNTRUTHS in the world of dogs.

Should you obtain a dog that has been prenamed (irrespective of age,) and it doesn't suit you — change it! The dog no longer belongs to your "cousin," he belongs to you.

Should you rename your dog and you can possibly make it close to the same tone as his prior name, (Majah to Major or Mariah to Maria,) that's nice, but if you can't go for it anyhow — HE/SHE ... IS ... YOUR ... DOG! As to the dog, he/she will get used to their new name in no time at all; and besides, he/she doesn't care what you call them — just so you don't call them, "late for dinner!"

One of our students named his Schipperkee/Shih-tzu mix, Skipshit. Whatever name **you** choose for your dog just remember to be reasonable and the affect that it could have on his personality or his temperment.

THE LIST OF NAMES

- A -

Aaron
Abby
Abigail
Ace
Acee
Adam
Adonis
A.J.
Akeelo
Akeila
Akita
Aladdin
Albert
Alex
Alexandra
Alfalfa
Alfie
Alpine
Aly
Amanda
Amber
Amos
Amy
Anna

Andre
Andy
Angel
Angus
Annie
Apache
Apollo
Army
Asha
Ashley
Asti
Astro
Atlas
Aussie
Autumn

- B -

B.A.
Baba
Babe
Baby
Bacardi
Badley
Baggins

Bahdgy
Bailey
Baja
Ballu
Bam Bam
Bandido
Bandit
Banjo
Barney
Baron
Baroness
Baron
Bart
Basia
Basil
Bauer
Baxter
B.B.
Bear
Beas
Bedsley
Beatrice
Beau
Beaudacios
Becky
Belle

Ben
Benji
Benny
Benson
Bentley
Berford
Bernadette
Bertie
Bianca
Bibbs
Biff
Biko
Bimba
Bing
Bingo
Binkie
Binky
Bismark
Bits
B.J.
Blackbeard
Blackie
Blaze
Blazer
Blitz
Blue
Blues

Blum
Bo
Bob
Bobe
Bobby
BoBo
Bogart
Bogie
Bonaparte
BonBon
Bonky
Bonnie
BooBoo
BooDah
Boogie
Booker
Boomer
Booney
Boots
Boris
Bosco
Boss
Boswell
Bosworth
Bowser
Bounder
Bozo

Brady
Brandon
Brandy
Braxton
Brett
Bridget
Brie
Brinkley
Britt
Brittany
Bronson
Brownie
Brunner
Bruno
Brutus
Bubba
Bubbles
Buck
Buckwheat
Bud
Buddha
Buddy
Buff
Bufford
Buffy
Bugsy
Bukshi

Bullet	Cess	Chief
Bullseye	Chamois	Chien
Bullwinkle	Champ	Chilly
Bumpy	Champagne	Chimmi
Buster	Chance	China
Butch	Chandler	Chino
Buttons	Chani	Chip
Byron	Chara	Chips
	Charity	Chiquita
- C -	Charles	Chiquito
	Charlie	Chispa
	Charlotte	Chloe
Cabo	Charmin	Choco
Caesar	Charo	Chocolate
Cain	Chase	Christa
Cairo	Chastity	Christine
Cali	Chauncey	Christy
Candy	Chavito	Chrome
Cappy	Checkers	Chubbs
Cara	Chelsea	Chutney
Carlie	Chesie	Cin-Cin
Carney	Chester	Cinco
Casey	Cheyenne	Cinder
Casha	Chiba	Cindy
Casper	Chica	Cinta
Cat	Chicklet	Cisko
C.C.	Chico	C.J.
Cecil		

Clay
Cleo
Clipper
Clover
Clyde
CoCo
Coconut
Codger
Cody
Colby
Colt
Conan
Conrad
Cookie
Cooper
Coquis
Corby
Corey
Corky
Corona
Coronel
Cosmo
Cossak
Coty
Countess
Courtney
Cricket

Cristina
Crockett
Cruiser
Crystal
Cubby
Cuda
Cuddles
Czar

- D -

Dae
Daisy
Daisy Mae
Dakota
Dallas
Damian
Dana
Danaz
Danger
Dani
Dante
Daphne
Darby
Darien
DeeDee
Delta

Demi
Dempset
DewDad
Dexter
Dharma
Diamond
Diana
DiDo
Diego
Digger
Dillinger
Dingo
Dinky
Ditto
Dixie
D.J.
Doby
D.O.G.
Doggie
Doll
Dollar
Dolly
Domingo
Dominick
Domino
Donatello
Donnie

Doogie
Droopy
Duba
Duchess
Dudley
Duke
Dumo
Duncan
Dustin
Dusty
Dylan
Dynah
Dynamo

- E -

Ebbo
Ebony
Einstein
Elke
Elika
Elsa
Elska
Elsie
Ellie
Elliot
Elvis

Emma
Eros
Escrow
Eskimo
Estee
E.T.
Evany

- F -

Fable
Fajita
Fairway
Faival Farsday
Farley
Fasha
Fawn
Fausto
Fido (was the
name of President
Lincoln's dog)
Fifi
Flanagan
Flosk
Floopy
Fluffy
Flurry

Flynn
Foxy
Francis
Frankie
Freckles
Fred
Freddy
Freeway
Frisco
Frisky
Fritter
Fritz
Frosty

- G -

Gabby
Gabriel
Galaxy
Garp
Garth
Gassie
Gator
George
Georgie Girl
Geronimo
Gerry

GiGi
Ginger
Ginny
Girlie
Gizmo
Glacier
Goldie
Goliath
Gordie
Grace
Greco
Greta
Gretchen
Gretel
Grizzly
Guardian
Gunnar
Gunny
Gunther
Gus
Gusto
Gyps
Gypsy

- H -

Hades

Haggar
Hallie
Hana
Hanak
Hannah
Happy
Harley
Harold
Harry
Hattie
Hawkeye
Heather
Heidi
Heihsiung
Heineken
Henderson
Henry
Hildie
Hildy
Hilo
Hobbs
Hobby
Hobie
Hogan
Holly
Honey
Hooch

Hoover
Hostess
Huma
Humbug
Humphrey
Hyme

- I -

Islay
Itchi
Izzy

- J -

Jack
Jackson
Jacques
Jade
Jaffa
Jaime
Jaice
Jake
James
Jamie
Jasmine
Jason

Jasper	Juno	Kelsey
Jay	Justin	Kena
Jaya		Kenji
Jaynie	**- K -**	Keno
Jazz		Khan
Jazzy	Kachar	Kiesha
J.D.	Kahlua	Kiki
Jedi	Kairo	Kiltie
Jenga	Kaiser	Kimbo
Jenny	Kal	Kimi
Jesse	Kalif	Kimo
Jessica	Karina	King
Jiggs	Karl	Kinobi
Jim	Kash	Kiowa
Jingles	Kate	Kiri
J.J.	Katie	Kiska
Joc	Kato	Kita
Joe	Katrina	Kiwi
Joey	Kayla	Kizhii
JoJo	Kaya	Kleo
Johann	Keann	Klondike
Josh	Keeah	Knickers
Joshua	Keesho	Knight
Julian	Kegger	Koala
Julie	Kegmo	Kodi
Juliet	Keisha	Kodiak
Julius	Kelly	Kody

Koko
Kona
Kooba
Korky
Krissy
Kristal
Kristie
K.T.
Kukla
Kuma
Kyid

- L -

Ladd
Lady
LadyCat
LadyDi
Laika
Laki
Landa
Larro
Laser
Laska
Lassie
Lassiter
Leca
Lechin

Lee
Lena
Leo
Leroy
Lexis
Lexy
Libby
Licorice
Lightning
Lily
Linc
Ling-Ling
Lita
Liza
Lobo
Lola
Lord
Lorean
Lori
Lottie
Louie
Louis Lipps
Lucia
Lucky
Luke
Lu
LuLu

Luna

- M -

Mac
Macho
Madison
Maggie
Magic
Magnum
Maina
Major
Mandy
Mariah
Margaret
Marley
Maverick
Maui
Max
Max-a-Million
Maxie
Maxim
Maxine
Maximillian
Maxwell
Maya
Maynard G.

McDuff	Mocha	Natasha
McMurphy	MoJo	Nathan
McTavish	Molly	Natops
Meche	Molsen	Nea
Megan	Mona	Neptune
Meka	Monty	Newton
Mel	Moon Dance	Nicholas
Mele	Moose	Nicky
Mercedes	Morley	Nicole
Michelle	Mr. Banks	Nigel
Mickey	Mr. T.	Nikki
Midnight	Muddee	Nikita
Mike	Muffin	Niko
Mikey	Mulligan	Nisky
Miko	MuMu	Nitro
Millwall	Munchkin	Noah
Milton	Murphy	Nooky
MiMi	Muzzy	Nora
Mindy		Norman
Ming	**- N -**	Nugget
Minnie		Nuschler
Minuit	Nadia	Nuska
Miss	Nally	
Missy	Nanook	**- O -**
Misty	Nanu	
Misty Sue	Nash	Oatmeal
Mitzi	Nasi	

Oblio
Ogi
Olga
Oliver
Ollie
O'Malley
Onyx
Orchid
Orejas
Oreo
Oricel
Ornery
Orville
Osa
Oscar
Osito
Oso
Ote
Otto
Ozzie

-P-

Paca
Pachca
Paddles

Paka
Palapa
Pamuk
Pancho
Panda
Pandora
Parker
Pasha
Paskey
Patches
Patience
Patsy Jane
Paula
P.D.
Peabo
Peaches
Peanuts
Pecs
Peluso
Penelope
Penny
Pepper
Peppermint
  Patty
Peppy
Perdy
Perra

Perry
Persia
Petey
Petry
Phantom
Phoebe
Pike
Pilot
Polar
Pongo
Poo
Pooch
Pooka
Poupe
Precious
Prieto
Prince
Princess
Princeton
Prissy
Pro
Promise
Pudge-
Chomper (Pudge
when he is nice –
'Chomper' when
he bites)

Puffer
Puglsey
Puppa
Putnam

- Q -

Quake
Quaxo
Queen
Quevo
Quincy
Quinneth

- R -

Raad
Racquie
Radar
Raffi
Raffles
Raider
Raija
Rainer
Rainy
Raisin
Rajah

Ralph
Rambo
Randi
Ranger
Rascal
Rebel
Rebound
Red
Redford
Regae
Regina
Rex
Rey
Ridget
Riker
Riley
Rio
Riva
R.J.
Roca
Rocco
Rochester
Rocket
Rocky
Rodin
Roman
Romeo

Roscoe
Roshi
Rosie
Rouge
Rowdy
Roxanne
Roxie
Ruby
Ruff & Reddy
Rufus
Rupert
Rusty

- S -

Saber
Sabrina
Sachi
Saco
Sadie
Saffy
Sage
Sahib
Sailor
Sake
Salinas

Sally	Shasta	Skipper
Sam	Shautsy	Skippy
Samantha	Sheeba	Skoshi
Sambo	Sheehan	Smidgen
Sampson	Sheena	Smith
Sandy	Sheild	Smokey
Sara	Shelby	Snickers
Sarge	Shelly	Snookey
Sasha	Shep	Snoopy
Sassy	Sherman	Snow
Savannah	Shiloh	Snow Ball
Scarlet	Shimshon	Snow Flake
Schatze	Shinook	Snuffy
Schultz	Shintel	Sonny
Scooter	Shujo	Sonny Bear
Scout	Sidney	Sonny Boy
SeaBreeze	Sierro	Sophie
Segart	Sig	Spanky
Senji	Silver	Sparky
Senor	Simba	Spencer
Sergeant	Sinjin	Sphritz
Shadow	Simon	Spike
Shakarr	Simone	Spriit
Shammie	Sir Garfield	Splosh
Shannon	Sirius	Spot
Shantee	Sister	Slpotze
Shasha	Skip	Spring

Springsteen   Tama   Tiko
Spud   Tanjy   Timber
Spunky   Tannah   Tina
Starbuck   Tarzon   Tiny
Stazi   Tasha   Tippy
Stella   Tashi   Tita
Stephanie   Tashia   Titano
Stormy   Tawnee   Tito
Streak   Taylor   T.J.
Studly   T-Bo   Toby
Sugar   Teddy   Tobby
Sukie   Tempe   Tomba
Summer   Tenann   Tooter
Sunny   Tequila   Tootsie
Sunshine   Terra   Toppy
Sunset   Terry   Tops
Sushi   Tessa   Toro
Suzy   Texas   Torrey
Sweet Pea   Theodore   Tosca
Sybil   Thor   Tosha
                 Thud   ToTo

- T -   Thunder   Touche
                 Tia   Toysi
Taffy   Tiffany   Travis
Tai   Tiger   Travler
Tai-Lo   Tiger Lily   Trevor
Take   Tiki   Trible

Triston
Trixie
Trouser
Tuck
Tucker
Tuki
Tuna
Tundra
Tuskin
Tuxedo
Twister
Tyan
Tyler
Tyson

- W -

Walter
Wendy
Wesson
Wheels
Whimpy
Whitney
Wicket
Widow
Wiggles

Willoughby
Willy
Winnie
Winston
Wolf
Wolfgang
Wolfie
Woody
WowWow
Wreckles
Wuffy

- U -

Uba

- V -

Vader
Val
Valentine
Velvet
Vincente
Vina
Viva
Vladimir
Volker

- Y -

Yakov
Yana
Yannie
Yaz
Yoda
Yogi
YoKo
Yoshi
Yuma
YumYum

- Z -

Zak
Zapa
Zelda
Zeus
Ziggy
Zimba
Zipper
Zoe
Zora
Zorro

HOUSEBREAKING ENCLOSURE

LUCY BENKLE
Your puppy's bed and place.

LESSON #001
HOUSEBREAKING AND MANAGING YOUR PUPPY
... OR OLDER DOG

In this lesson we parallel training the baby puppy dog to rearing a human baby, and other situations which apply to the human in general.

To the students at the school being trained with their puppies, we ask the following questions, which we now ask you:

Say that you have just been blessed with the arrival of your human baby. When you brought him home from the hospital, would you take the human baby and set him on the living room floor and say, "Welcome, Baby! This is your home, this is your living room, and if you get hungry, the refrigerator is in the kitchen and the kitchen is..." and so on and so forth. Would you do that with the human baby? Of course not! When you think about it, how is it any different when you bring home the baby puppy dog?

Isn't it true, that when you brought the human baby home, in order to protect him from himself, especially when he began to crawl, (i.e. to keep him from pulling the lamps on top of himself, putting his little fingers into the electric outlets, falling down the stairs, etc.), isn't it true, that one of the family members had to watch him virtually 100% of the time? When you think about it, how is that any different from the baby puppy dog? Isn't it also true that it's almost impossible to keep your eye on the human baby 100% of the time (family members must shower, take care of other personal needs, etc.) In order to protect the human baby during that time, where did we place him? Did we put him outside in the back yard, in the garage, or in the basement? No, of course not! We put the human baby into his baby bed or his play pen, where he feels secure and is protected from himself and outside forces.

WHEN WE THINK ABOUT IT . . .

A. In the classic movie "A Christmas Story," a most humorous scene was depicted. While at dinner, the baby of the family did not want to eat his dinner – a very full plate of cabbage, meat loaf and mashed potatoes. With mother's encouragement and words to the effect, "Come on sweetheart, be mommy's little piggy. How do the piggies do it? Come on, eat your dinner, do it for mommy. Show me how the piggies do it." And with this encouragement and father's obvious look of disgust and restraint, the young child picked up his plate and *stuffed, licked, and slobbered* his dinner...all over! **He all but made a pig of himself.**

Though humorous in the story, is this the way we normally feed our human babies? Do we let them *stuff, lick, and slobber* their food at any time that they want to? Isn't it true that, in order to adjust/train his untrained system, we put the human baby on a strict, supervised feeding schedule?

B. When the human baby wasn't wearing a diaper and he soiled himself, the carpet, or dad and mother's brand new comforter, did we rub his nose into his own mess?

"Z." When the human baby manages to pull the tablecloth off the table and break all the dishes, or other actions such as this, do we spank the baby with a rolled-up newspaper? Do we spank him...period?

...HOW IS ALL THIS DIFFERENT FROM THE BABY PUPPY DOG?

TRAINING

I personally consider a dog, in most aspects, not much different than a human being – in most cases, what applies to one, applies to the other. With this in mind, let us be **fair, kind, loving and use good judgment and common sense** when housebreaking our baby puppy dog.

Housebreaking means more than just teaching the baby puppy not to soil in the house, it also means teaching him to be an acceptable member of the family and not a juvenile delinquent!

The "A" through "Z" Housebreaking Steps are divided into four major categories:
    I. Your Puppy's Bed and Place
    II. Feeding
    III. Bathroom Training (The "Actual" House
        Rules)
    IV. Managing Your Puppy

I. YOUR PUPPY'S BED AND PLACE

A. When you first bring the puppy home **avoidance** is the best medicine. To avoid temptations when he is out and about, chew-proof and baby-proof your home as much as possible, and **do not** give him the run of the house.

B. Provide the puppy with a **secure** place (within the home if possible) that he will learn to recognize as entirely his own – this will be his "crib," his "playpen."

C. The dog is a social animal, therefore it's important to avoid prolonged periods of isolation. The dog appreciates his family and wants to be near them. **The place** that you provide for him should be one where he can readily see you in some of your daily routines.

D. The place that you provide should be a **tiled** area. If not, purchase a cut-to-fit piece of linoleum from your local home improvement/hardware store.

E. The size of the area that you provide should be 4' x 6' to 6' x 8'. This depends on the size that your particular puppy will grow to – small, medium, or large.

F. The sides of the puppy's place can be made out of 2 x 2's or 2 x 4's, plywood and heavy-gauge chicken wire. The chicken wire should be used on the side(s) where the puppy can easily see you in your daily routine.

G. Be sure that the height of the puppy's place is high enough to contain him as he grows – otherwise, a top should be provided. If a top is provided, it should be high enough that when the puppy has reached his full height (at approximately 6 to 8 months) he doesn't have to slouch when standing.

H. Cover the puppy's **entire** area with overlapping 3 or 4 sheets of newspaper. **This is not meant to teach the puppy to go to the bathroom in the house.**

There are **only** two purposes for their use:

1. To make it easier for you to clean-up should the puppy go to the bathroom in his area.

2. To emergency train the puppy to go on newspaper, should you not be available to take him outside to his bathroom when he has to go. This will probably be the case in most instances.

I. In the puppy's area maintain:

1. **His bedding.** Preferably something that can be easily washed; placed in the rear of the enclosure.

2. **His water dish.** So that the puppy can't tip it over or chew it, obtain one that is heavy-duty and heavy; ceramic/clay types are the best.

3. **Toys which are chew-safe.** Obtain a recommendation from your local pet store. You can't provide enough toys for your dog, especially when he has the run of the house and yard. Trust me when I tell you this – these toys will be deterrents and protection for your home and other priceless and meaningful possessions. **Provide your dog with lots and lots of toys.**

Should you catch your puppy chewing on objects other than his toys, correct him with a firm, "NOOOOO!" Move him away, and hand him one of his toys.

J. Regarding the puppy's bed area, if possible, but **not totally necessary**, provide a dog crate. This will simulate his den and should be big enough to accommodate the puppy when full grown. Within the enclosure, leave the crate's front door **off** and place his bedding in it. **Do not force** the puppy to go into it – just place it in his area. In most cases, the puppy **on his own** will learn to love it. You will find this to be a plus factor because you will naturally take advantage of it in many situations. If you notice the puppy not using the crate, try feeding him in it – he'll soon get the idea.

A dog crate or cage can be obtained from most pet stores. If you obtain a wire-type, place a blanket around it to provide more of a den atmosphere. Be sure to thoroughly tuck in or tape the sides of the blanket to keep the puppy from chewing and/or pulling it off.

K. The King Size Cage Method

Many of our students have used a king size wire-type cage (approximately 3 1/2' wide by 4 1/2' long and 3' tall) and have been very successful with housebreaking.

THE KING SIZE CAGE METHOD

- Place the cage where the family's main activities take place.
- Leave the cage door open when, under your supervision, the dog is out and about.

Aaron & Lia's, Jack Russell Terrier, Fletch, shows us his prettier north-side – on the next page he shows us his not-so-pretty south-side. When asked about his giant cage, "I love it!"

THE KING SIZE CAGE METHOD

- Take your dog outside to the bathroom on a regular schedule.
- Except at night, don't close your dog in the cage for more than 3 hours.

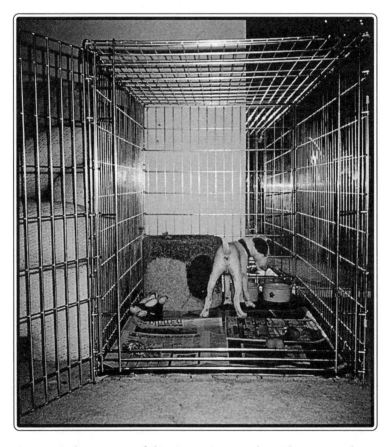

"I stay in here most of the time – it's my den. Please note that in my giant cage I have newspapers for any emergencies, my bed, food and water dishes...and lots of toys!"

The more successful ones were those who:

1. Placed the cage where the family's main activities took place.

2. Made it a **priority** to take their dog outside to the bathroom on a **very regular** schedule – every 2 hours during the day. Newspapers were not used.

3. Left the cage door open when the dog was out and about, under their supervision of course, so that the dog could go in and out at its discretion. A blanket or pillow was used as the dog's bed.

4. With the exception of during the night, never closed the dog in the cage for more than 3 hours.

5. Someone was at home almost 100% of the time.

You may want to try this method, most dogs love the king size cage.

L. We know you're tempted, but – **do not** be in a hurry to give the puppy the run of the house or to let him sleep with you until he is totally housebroken. Housebroken means that he can be trusted in all areas (approximately 6 months to a year old).

NOTE: Letting the puppy sleep with you is not recommended. However, experience has shown that irrespective of how much advice is given on this matter, many of us will allow the practice. With this in mind, we recommend – **you** are the leader of the pack, **you** can make any exceptions – we simply suggest to at least wait until the puppy **is** housebroken; *otherwise picture your bed as his bathroom!*

M. The puppy **must be** confined to his area virtually a 100% of the time. The exceptions are **only** when he is under **your** watchful eye and **your** direct supervision:

1. When you take him to his bathroom area.

2. During play, and during exercise periods.

To keep your puppy more tranquil during longer periods of your absence and at night, place in his bedding a loud ticking clock (representing the mother's heartbeat) or a hot water bottle wrapped in a small blanket. A radio playing near his area will also help. I'll kiddingly suggest to the students to be sure to pick a station he really likes. It's best to choose a station where there's a lot of talking.

"Z." To housebreak, beagle, Lucy Benkle (see photo at beginning of chapter), her "parents" chose to share with her part of their kitchen. Note how easily they prepared the 6' x

3 1/2' area for her. They knew it didn't have to be a penthouse!

1. The area **faces** the living room where most of the human activity takes place.

2. The front gate was easily made of wire and old pieces of lumber. It slides open and closed behind the refrigerator.

3. To protect the closet door on the left side, they used an old wooden door. To protect the cupboard door handles in the back of the enclosure, they placed a card table in front of them.

4. To cover the right side, an old plywood chalkboard was used.

5. Note the crate with the pillow in it which is the puppy's bed; food and water dishes; and lots and lots of toys.

6. Lucy's parents **didn't** use the newspaper method because they were at home the majority of the time and were able to take the puppy outside to her bathroom on a regular schedule – every 2 hours during the day, first thing in the morning, and last thing at night.

II. FEEDING

A. Remember that what goes in must come out! **No tid-bits** (treats) during housebreaking.

B. Feed the puppy on a **strict schedule**. The best schedule is one that best **fits your schedule – your daily routine**. After he's a year old, experience tells us that the best time to feed your dog is in the morning. This is probably when there will be the least amount of change to your schedule, in contrast to owners who feed after they get home from work, when delays are sure to occur. You'll find that feeding in the morning will be best for both of you because you won't have to "rush home" from work, a meeting, or a party; and your dog won't have to "starve half to death!"

C. Do not free-feed if at all possible. Three times a day until 6 months, two times a day until 1 year, and once a day thereafter is a normal feeding schedule for most dogs. However, your veterinarian's recommendation should also be sought.

As to the amount that you feed your puppy or grown dog, use the recommendations provided by the food makers on their bags. You'll find that in most cases the amounts are more than sufficient, and for some dogs, you may have to reduce their recommended amounts. Consult with your veterinarian.

D. Feeding should take place in the puppy's enclosure near his bedding. Place the food down and leave it for no more than 20 minutes. If he doesn't eat it, put it away until the next feeding schedule. Otherwise, it would be like free-feeding – and remember that if this is the case, he will eat a little bit and go a little bit, eat a little bit and go a little bit, and so on...you may never get him housebroken.

E. Feeding the dog human food is another area in the dog world that is not highly recommended – and – **this is** the ideal! However, we know that regardless of instructions, exceptions to this will be made. I hereby confess that I'm just as guilty. I **can not** "throw the first stone." I have always fed my dogs a quarter of a hot dog cut in little pieces and mixed with their every meal. If I have chicken for dinner, they get little pieces of chicken; if I have steak for dinner, they get little pieces of steak; and guess what they get for Thanksgiving and Christmas? Turkey is one thing my dogs have always loved. I know I am being silly, but, my personal justification has always been, how would I like it if **my** every meal consisted of corn flakes?

I might add that when mixing their food, I also add a little bit of very hot water to lightly moisten dry food. You may want to try this formula with your dog – they love it! And, I further confess, that in the case of my dogs, seldom (if ever) do I have to wash their dishes; when they get through eating, their dishes are...**clean!** I just rinse them.

If you are one to make the exception of feeding human food to your dog we simply suggest to use good judgment.

Wait until the puppy is at least 6 months old. Avoid feeding directly from the dining room table or directly out of the refrigerator. **DO NOT give your dog bones!!!**

F. For obvious reasons – **do not** disturb the puppy or grown dog while he is eating, **do not** create a situation which makes him become defensive over **his** food. This is not the time to toy with any dog. Defense mechanisms over our food are no less inherent in dogs than they are in humans. As we ask our students, we ask you: Say that you just started eating your dinner and someone came along and shoved or kicked you away from it. What would **you** do...or at least feel like doing? **Let** the "feeding-hour" for your dog be a "happy-hour!"

G. If you have two dogs **always** separate them during the feeding-hour.

H. Feeding time is just another time when we humans **do not** have to be **macho.** A prospective student quizzed me about teaching his 18 month old Rottweiler not to growl at his 6 year old little girl, "...as he did last night when she tried to take his food while he was eating." No matter how much I explained to this "gentleman" that there are right ways and wrong ways, especially regarding his children, his last words to me were, "If we feed it, we **damned well** better be able to take it away from him!"

Let the "feeding-hour" for your dog be a "happy-hour!" Leave him alone. **PERIOD.**

"**Z.**" Experience tells us that the majority of dogs that have bitten children (and adults, especially men) were dogs that the child or adult knew, not necessarily strays. All of us, including children, should be taught **safety** when dealing with dogs. We don't have to be afraid of dogs—especially our own—but the dog must be treated with respect, the same as we treat our human friends. We **don't** pull or bite their ears, poke at their eyes, disturb them while they're eating or sleeping, try to take food from them, pin them down, or aggressively kick them, etc.

What you would not do to a human friend, do not do to a dog friend!

Why put yourself, your family, your children, your friends and neighbors in harms-way? Under **no** circumstances is that necessary. Teach children safety rules around dogs. Apply sound common sense, good judgement, and remember that a dog is a dog, is a dog, is a dog, and will always be a dog. **PERIOD!** By the same token, do not put **the dog** in harms-way.

III. BATHROOM TRAINING
(THE "ACTUAL HOUSE RULES)

A. The puppy's bathroom area should be approximately 4' x 4' to 6' x 8' – again, depending on the size that he'll grow to.

1. Ideally, the area should be bordered with 2 x 2's or 2 x 4's, and **away** from the house.

2. The area **must** be kept clean at all times. The exception is only at the beginning of training, leave a little of his feces to create "a draw."

Regarding this, we ask our students: If we humans go to a bathroom and find that it's not flushed and a filthy mess, what do we do? We go someplace else, don't we? It's the same with the dog!

B. Take the puppy outside to his bathroom area:

1. First thing in the morning.
First thing in the morning means **first thing** in the morning. Think about it, what do we humans usually do first thing in the morning?

2. Last thing at night.

Last thing at night means **last thing** at night. You can not take the puppy outside at 8:00, 9:00 or 10:00, then watch the late late show, fix a midnight snack, go to the bathroom and then to bed. Because just about then, what do you suppose the puppy has to do? Last thing at night means **last thing at night.**

3. Five minutes after eating.

4. After he has been napping, playing, or exercising.

C. To the puppy, until he is **absolutely** housebroken, going outside should mean only one thing: **going to the bathroom.** Do not play with him or let him romp around in his bathroom area.

1. **Taking the puppy to the bathroom means taking him to the bathroom. Do not just open the door leading to his bathroom and expect him to go on his own.**

2. When taking the puppy to his bathroom area, always use the same path and the same doorway. To represent a happy time for him, be exuberant as you take him, but remain passive while he's going.

D. Because going to the bathroom for the puppy is a

very private thing to do, do not expect him to go *on command*. Picture this scenario: We take our puppy to his bathroom area, and there we stand, towering over him, commanding, "Okay puppy, go to the bathroom. Go on! Go to the bathroom." Given this same scenario, would you go to the bathroom? Once you have the puppy in his bathroom area, turn your head and ignore him for 3 to 5 minutes. Let him do his thing. When he is fully done (you'll know), **passively** praise him and immediately take him back in the house. If after 5 minutes, he doesn't go, (you don't have to wait until "hell freezes over!") He obviously doesn't have the need to go at this time. Take him back into the house; he'll have to wait until the next outing.

E. Don't make a grandiose display of praise when your puppy does relieve himself. Many that have, have implanted in their dogs the idea that going to the bathroom pleases us ever so much that they repeat the performance over and over – *when, and wherever.* **Be passive** in your praise for him. "Oh...good puppy, good puppy." Then romp him back to the house.

F. Another area where over-exuberance in praise also has been known to hinder is when through that same emphatic praise we interrupt the puppy from finishing. Picture this: The puppy begins to squat, and immediately we clap our hands as we exclaim, "Oh, good dog, good dog!" Then we take him back into the house, and a few minutes later, guess what? **He finishes!**

G. Newspaper Removal:

1. During the housebreaking period, remove soiled papers in the puppy's area immediately as noticed and replace with fresh ones. **Do not** leave any area of the floor exposed.

2. A puppy's tendency is to soil away from where they eat and sleep. Therefore, after two weeks of complete coverage, every third or fourth day, expose a one foot square area of the floor starting from the back proceeding to the front, by removing one section of newspaper until such time that the entire area is exposed.

3. If the puppy has an *accident* on the exposed area of the floor or outside of his area, wash thoroughly and rinse with a solution of 1 part vinegar to 2 parts water.

4. If you see the puppy begin to have an accident on the floor outside of his area, immediately correct him with a firm, "NO!" and take him outside to his bathroom. Praise him when he does relieve himself outside, but **not** *during*. Wait until he is thoroughly done.

I asked 9-year-old Evan of Alvarado Estates in San Diego, "What do most people do when their dog goes to the bathroom in the house?" Without batting an eye and as his mother's face flushed, Evan responded, "Get the maid of course."

5. If the puppy keeps missing the newspaper after you have exposed most of the floor in his area – he does not yet have the idea. Go back to square one. Cover the entire area again and start over.

6. To ensure against future accidents after housebreaking, maintain a single section of newspaper in "his area."

NOTE: If there's someone in your home who can take the puppy outside to his bathroom every two hours throughout the day, you don't need to use the newspapers for housebreaking.

H. Your puppy will **first** be housebroken, as it relates to going to the bathroom, when he will wait to go until you take him to his bathroom area or signal you by running to the door, whining, or – *cross his legs and squint or roll his teary eyes.* Don't worry, you'll learn to recognize his signal. Many students have felt that this is the time to give the puppy the run of the house – **DON'T!** Not only can the puppy revert, but he may also start *marking* the territory, not to mention the development of other not-so-pleasant habits (getting into the trash, chewing, digging, etc.).

For some unknown reason, many students insist on being in a hurry to give their dog the run of the house. I ask them, "What do you suppose your puppy, even after he grows up, is going to do 90% of the time, especially while you are gone? Is he going to run the vacuum, do the laundry, or fix dinner for you?" Ninety percent of the time the dog is going to sleep. How much room does he really need for this! **Do not** give the dog the run of the house until he is **fully** housebroken – six months to one year.

Many students have asked, "How long will it take to fully housebreak my puppy?" To this, there is no exact answer; it's like asking how long it will take a human baby to be potty trained. I have seen some dogs that accomplish it in a matter of days, some months, and I have seen many (especially the toy-types) that at 5 years old are still going to the bathroom in the house or ripping the newspapers, carpeting and everything that they can get their teeth into. Generally speaking, most puppies will probably be housebroken (as it relates to going to the bathroom), by the time you get to the removal of the last section of newspaper in his area. However, he still can not be trusted with free-run of the house.

"Z". Being a puppy parent carries a great deal of responsibility and there are many needs that must be attended to. As each human's schedule is different, we suggest that not all the rules explained here are set in cement. **You** are the leader of the pack. **You** can make any exception or adjustment you desire to fit your particular needs and schedule. We simply encourage you to have **patience and use common sense**. If in doubt regarding any instructions or needs, check with your veterinarian. Remember that in most cases, what applies to the human baby, applies to the baby puppy dog.

IV. MANAGING YOUR PUPPY

A. The previous strict guidelines...and common sense, are – **the order of the day!**

B. Do not ever pin your puppy down – or any part of him. See tid-bit "P" Lesson 101. To get him used to your **holding** him, do it in small steps, and give him lots of praise and assurance.

C. If your puppy "throws a tantrum" when he's placed in his playpen, **ignore** him as best you can, and don't cause him to **train you by drawing you** every time he whimpers. **I assure you**, that if you ignore him, he will get the idea that it doesn't do him any good – and in most cases he will be quiet, settle down, and go to sleep.

"**Z.**" If your puppy nips or bites you (it's usually the hands), maneuver your hand so that you grab the lower jaw (preferably with your thumb in his mouth and on top of his tongue); squeeze and hold him for a few seconds while he squirms to get away. Release the squeeze – he will pull away – but don't **you** pull your hand away, **make him retreat!**

If he immediately comes back to bite again, grab him and squeeze a little harder, and hold him a little longer. You can also **shockingly flick** his nose with your finger every time he bites, at the same time you command, "NO!" or "NOOOOOO!"

If the puppy bites other parts of your body (such as your feet), as he is biting and in a shocking manner, move that part of your body **into him** – **make him back-off, make him retreat! Remember that shock does not mean hurt.** Each time that the puppy backs-off—retreats—you should come back with a little passive verbal praise, "YOU BE A GOOD PUPPY – GOOOOD PUPPY!" If he continues his challenge and/or gets too rowdy, simply put him back into his playpen until he calms down.

WORDS OF CAUTION

It would take a book the size of Dr. Spock's Baby Book to enumerate all the areas where **caution** is in order when it comes to your puppy. However, these three **ABC's** are noteworthy:

A. A WORD OF CAUTION REGARDING PUPPY EXERCISE

Though jogging and other vigorous exercise may be good for you, it is not the best for your puppy. Damage which shows up later in life could occur. Not even long walks should be forced on him. As with the human baby – will he be forced to do push-ups, lift weights, and run for a mile? Of course not! As with the human baby, let the baby dog obtain his exercise in natural ways through play periods. As your dog grows up, consult your veterinarian regarding vigorous and/or strenuous exercise. Please do remember that **caution** should be the order of the day. As my friend, Clark L. Kelly, D.V.M., suggests, "As we are watchful of our children's **tolerance** level, be watchful of your dog's tolerance level and **do not push them** past it."

B. A WORD OF CAUTION REGARDING PUPPY OBEDIENCE AND BEHAVIOR TRAINING

Please see Tid-Bit G, Lesson 101, A Through Z Tid-Bits to Ponder and Remember.

C. A WORD OF CAUTION REGARDING PUPPY SOCIALIZATION

At the early stages of life a puppy is **very** responsive to **any** stimulus and, therefore, can be highly influenced both positively and negatively. Many puppies that experience trauma at an early age retain those experiences for the rest of their life and as they grow, they develop an introverted personality. This is where dogs that are known as "fear-biters" come into play. They bite not because by nature they are aggressive, but because they are fearful. On the other hand, puppies that have been **carefully socialized** and are free of trauma, grow up to be friendly, responsive and outgoing.

Socialization **is** very important for puppies, but because of their **acute** responsiveness to outside forces, it is highly recommended that during socialization, owners emphasize the positive and **be very watchful of matters that could traumatize them** – remember their susceptibility to shock. Another important point to keep in mind is that they have not been fully immunized. **Once again, what you would not do with the human baby, do not do with the baby dog.**

HOUSEBREAKING AND MANAGING YOUR OLDER DOG

As the years have gone by, I can not even begin to tell you the number of calls that we receive at the school inquiring about housebreaking the older dog.

To people who have had their dogs for any length of time, especially since puppyhood, I assure them that **in most of these cases**, it's no longer a matter of housebreaking, because the dog already knows not to go to the bathroom in the house. More than likely it's a matter of *marking* his territory. "Who is the leader of the pack?" I might add, that dogs **do** mark by doing *number one* or *number two*. In any event, the problem has to be solved.

To housebreak an older dog, simply follow the same basic rules that have been outlined in this chapter; especially as they relate to supervision, confinement and his outdoor "bathroom area". Take him regularly to this area, **just as if he were a puppy**. Remember to emphasize obedience and behavior training.

Do not hesitate to shame your dog when he goes to the bathroom anywhere other than in the correct place. Emphatically show your displeasure and total disapproval. Do this by casually taking him to "the scene of the crime;" put his nose near (**never in**) his *mess,* and hold him there for about five seconds as you command, "This is a NO! NO! NO! NO! NO! ... NO!" Then, turn him loose and give a little **passive** love, "You **be** a good dog!" And ignore him for a while.

NOTE: These instructions are **only** for an older dog, not a puppy!

Let me share with you rules that we use to housebreak guide dogs at the school for the blind. Rules that you may want or should use with your older dog.

When the guide dog is placed with his new blind master, in most cases, the dog is not yet totally housebroken. Remember that for a great part of his young life, while being trained, he lived in a kennel with other guide dog trainees. When the guide dog completes his guidance, obedience and behavior training and graduates, he is placed with his new blind master with whom he will spend the rest of his days – almost 100% of the time. Under the watchful eye of a trainer/instructor, the blind master will, for the first four to six weeks, provide all the supervision of his new guide dog; then he is totally on his own.

To ensure housebreaking of his new guide dog prior to taking him home, the dog is taken to his bathroom area first thing in the morning, last thing at night, after eating and before and after each of their many training walks. If the dog goes to the bathroom in any area other than his designated place, he is corrected and shamed, as previously explained.

During the night, the dog is placed beside the blind master's bed on a two foot chain tie down, which is affixed to an eyebolt at the wall's baseboard. The dog is also placed there any other time when he is not under the direct supervision of his blind master – such as when his master is in the shower, shaving, dressing, etc. Following these **strict guidelines** and **tie-down confinement**, the guide dog is housebroken in no time at all. I might add that after just a few weeks, in most cases, the tie-down is no longer necessary. The dog will know and get to love his place and stay there all night or any other time that he is commanded to do so.

Many of our students at ABC School for Dogs have used this same method with their lay dogs and have reported nothing but...MIRACULOUS RESULTS!

TID-BITS TO PONDER AND REMEMBER

A. Confinement, avoidance and supervision.

B. What you would not do to a human friend, **do not do** to a dog friend!

C. What applies to the baby human, in most cases applies to the baby dog **and it's a labor of love!**

"Z." **Do not** be in a hurry to give your dog the run of the house until he is **fully housebroken.**

THANK YOU

"We are elated with all the training we received at ABC School for Dogs. Not only for Fletch's outstanding housebreaking, obedience and behaviour training, but the knowledge that we acquired in learning how to handle him. We are a happy family! David you are the greatest – as Fletch loves you, we love you!"

Aaron, Lia and Fletch Silverman
San Diego, California

DIANA DEAN AND PRINCE
Lemon Grove, California

After the "ABC's" Prince quickly shed his very rough coat.

LESSON #101
A THROUGH Z
TID-BITS TO PONDER AND REMEMBER!

A s to who is smarter and who trains who to do what, are everyday questions in the world of dog training.

This lesson is designed to give you an overview of the more important dog training tid-bits, thus you will definitely become smarter than your dog; and through your smarter training efforts, your dog will definitely be "A...Better...Canine!"

TID-BITS TO PONDER AND REMEMBER

A. Do you like to by nagged? Does your spouse? Do your children? **Neither does your dog!** How many times have you heard people say to their dogs, or been guilty of yourself: "No, dog! No, dog! No, dog!" Time after time, hour, day, week, month, year after year, we say, "No, dog! Pleeease, dog! You are driving me crazy!" Then one or two years go by, and...guess what? The puppy is no longer a puppy! Now he is a **moose**, and he is **no good!**

When they reach this point, what do people do with many of their dogs? Let's here and now face the unfortunate facts. Some will kick them, some will kick them...**out!** Some will drop them off in the countryside and many simply end up at the pound! If no one claims or adopts them, what eventually happens? Is this really fair to the dog? **Whose fault was it anyhow?** I rest my case! In commanding your dog, if he doesn't respond the first time – **teach** him, but **do not...nag** him! Be **reasonable** as to what you expect from your dog. "Out of the mouths of babes," this young man wasn't being facetious when he asked, "Can the dog be taught to go fart in another room?"

Don't put your dog in harms-way. Veterinarians will tell you of problems that can afflict dogs if they are forced to jog for too long. Problems such as heart conditions, heat prostration, foot and pad injuries, and arthritis. The human may be able to run for miles on end, but not the dog, especially if he is under two years old. A couple of reasons for this is that dogs don't perspire well, and they require more rest and water stops than humans. Unfortunately, I all too often see people taking their puppies and dogs out for a jog. The dog, with his little butt hugging the sidewalk, is panting and wondering, "Why this cruel and unusual punishment?" I quote my friend, Clark L. Kelly, D.V.M., **"As we are watchful of our children's tolerance level, be watchful of your dog's tolerance level and do not push them past it."**

B. If you can read, understand, learn and follow **ABC** directions, you **can** train your own dog! We encourage you to **slowly** read this book from cover to cover and then apply the instructions, **explicitly as given**, one lesson at a time. Dog training is not just dog training, it is first and foremost – people training.

C. As it is with the human, be it a child or an adult who is attending school, it is **the same** for the dog:

1. The setting should at all times be **conducive** to learning.
2. Learning sessions should be kept to a **reasonable** time period.
3. Before advancing to another lesson, give **ample time** for the dog to fully understand and be able to perform the current lesson.

D. With the above points kept in mind:

1. Training sessions with your dog should, at first,

not be in a carnival-type setting; with many adults, children and/or dogs all around. First, have him learn – then, expose him to the "combat zone!" Remember that our dogs do not live in parks, in parking lots, or with a bunch of other dogs. They live in homes with people. Therefore, the training setting should preferably be in the same type of setting.

2. Keep training sessions to maneuvers which take a maximum of twenty minutes.

3. Give the dog a **minimum** of one week practice to the current lesson before advancing him to the next lesson. At ABC School for Dogs, we give **two** weeks between lessons.

4. Bear in mind that we're just **beginning** training, so do yourself and your dog the biggest favor possible: **To control him until he his fully trained and trustworthy, provide him with a kennel.** Outside if he's large—otherwise it's your choice—but **do not** give him the run of your home or yard. Use good judgement and common sense regarding its size and location. Believe me, the expense and effort that you'll incur will be negligible compared to the expense, effort, frustration and discomfort that you are sure to experience should you not provide him with a kennel. During the first year or

better, while you're away or not directly supervising your dog, he should be confined and controlled.

E. The methods taught in this book are precisely the ones used by "real" professional trainers, both in the public eye (such as in the training of Guide Dogs for the blind) and in the privacy of their training establishments. As unfortunately has been the case in many situations, these methods are not meant to soft-pedal the issues of training by taking advantage of and playing on overzealous human sentimentalities.

Many men and women fail to complete armed forces boot-camp because of separation anxieties from home – one's family, daddy or mommy. This happens to dogs, especially little ones, and many have even died from it. **Don't** spoil your dog so rotten that he goes through life an emotional invalid; that when you must go away for a few days and place him in a kennel, he goes bananas. Teach him from puppyhood that he must learn to stand his ground. **Love him, but don't kill your dog...with kindness!**

F. "Dave, just how smart is the dog, anyhow?" This is one of the questions that has been asked by students more than most. When answering, I always pause, as I quizzically and slowly look up to them and respond,

"Well...you see...the question really **is not**...how smart
is **the dog...!**"

**G. There is no such thing as "Puppy Obedience
Classes." Do not be taken in!** For up to at least the
first four months, let the puppy be a "puppy!" Let him
have a little fun. He'll have to grow up soon enough!
To control him at the beginning, use good judgment,
i.e., proper confinement when you can't keep your eye
on him; chew proof your home and the area where
you keep him; provide adequate toys and...overall, **be
patient with him.** Remember that he is, after all – **a
puppy!** Besides cruel owners, if there is one thing that
upsets me in this business, it is quote, trainers, unquote,
who play on the unsuspecting sentimentalities of the
human by offering puppy classes. **There is no such
thing! Do not be taken in!**

There have been more dogs who experienced
trauma through puppy classes, which at a later age created distortions in their nature. One such case was Sasha,
a little female German Shepherd, imported from Germany, owned by a lady about 65 and living alone. Because the puppy was jumping and chewing on her and
the furniture, etc., the trainer she hired suggested methods of correction which should only be reserved for
more mature dogs. When I was called to the case, at the

golden age of only six months, the dog was already irreversibly neurotic. The dog had to be put to sleep. **And this is only one case!**

I pray that the information contained in this book will enlighten many to be "real" and allow the dog and its world their fair and deserving place.

In discussing so-called puppy obedience classes with a new Rottweiler owner—a family with two children, two- and four-years-old—they stated that their breeder suggested that from the very beginning, each time the puppy is fed, have the children sit by the puppy's bowl, and to even encourage them to play with the dog's food while he's eating.

I couldn't believe my ears! I really wanted to explode on this one! At times, I have been known to have a "little bit" of a temper...but don't you believe it! It's really all an act. I must remember to be tactful and diplomatic. So...I swallowed hard and suggested that they do as their conscience dictates. However, I also shared the following story with them.

This is what Dr. and Mrs. Staples experienced when they obtained an eight-week-old German Shepherd puppy, Duke. For years they had two Pugs, Shorty and

Snotty. From the first day of Duke's arrival, they allowed all three to eat out of the same bowl. All was fine for the first seven months – no problems. Shorty and Snotty could at anytime go to the food bowl while Duke was eating. But in the eighth month, Shorty went to the bowl while Duke was eating – for the last time. Duke took but one bite out of Shorty, and popped his eyes right out of his head. The vet tried to save the little Pug, but to no avail. Two months later, Snotty experienced the same fate.

I paused for a moment before stating, that "this doesn't necessarily mean that this is what will happen in each and every case. But, you do as your conscience dictates."

In our Housebreaking Lesson #001, we paralleled a "baby puppy" to a "baby human being." **There is not much difference!** Much care, much love, much guidance, much patience is needed! It's true that a puppy at eight or nine weeks can begin to learn, but few humans have the stamina, patience and know-how that is required. If guidance is needed, consult your veterinarian or a professional trainer – check credentials and success stories and satisfied clients that he/she is bound to have if he/she is a true professional. Generally speaking, **let the puppy be a puppy.**

When training your puppy or dog, always remember that there are facts...and there are opinions – and opinions are like belly-buttons, everybody has one! The hurt and damage that has been done by opinions to dogs and their owners trying to do "the right thing" is unbelievable and incomprehensible. Opinions from "experts" running the entire gamut. Experts who should know better – from **"professional"** trainers to **"humane"** treatment animal control investigators to legislators– opinions so cockeyed they would even make Little Red Riding Hood's, Lobo, run...**away from home!**

H. A space or pause between your dog's name and the desired command is very important. Do not cause your dog, as so many have, to think that his first name is "Fido" and his last name is "Heel." Have you ever heard of

"Fido heel!" or "Fido no!" I had a little old lady student (not from Pasadena) once tell me, "I know what you mean, Dave, my dog thinks his name is Fidogetoutofthetrash!"

I. The **frequent** use of your dog's name and **tones** he enjoys is very important. "Prince is a **good boy!** Prince likes to have **dinner.** He likes to **chase the ball.** He likes to **play** with **Honey,** (Prince's female companion), and...he likes **cookies!** Prince **is** a little **angel** dog!"

This will make him feel very good and cause him to know that he, in fact, is an acceptable member of the family pack. I have always done this with my dogs, and in response, the way they wiggle, and smile, and go around and around, you'd think that they'd crawl right out of their skins! The pleasure and the bond that you'll derive with your dog, as I have – with **ALL** the dogs in my life – is **invaluable** and **immeasurable!**

J. Bones...of any kind (rawhides excepted) **are not good for your dog.** Although your dog loves them and loves you for giving them to him – they are **not** good for him! How many times have we seen dogs at the "ripe ol' age" of five or six years without teeth. Why? Not to mention all the unnecessary bone-related veterinarian expenses.

K. Dogs do not learn anything by beating them. They learn only through **leadership,** the **shock** factor and the **love** factor. One of the main reasons why many humans end-up with dogs that literally dominate the household is that they are unwilling to **correctly** correct their dog – thinking that they are going to hurt him.

NEVER LEAVE TWO UNTRAINED PUPPIES ALONE IN THE HOUSE!

"Puppies!!" See next page.

NO MORE MISDEEDS

Dawn Ketcham, Sasha and Snow Bear
Springfield, Virginia

At the beginning of training, I always ask the students, "Do you want a well trained dog? Well...there are no two ways about it – you **must** be willing to correct him – **correctly and consistently.**

L. Why should the dog not think that he owns you? Are we not the ones to emphasize our subservience to him? Think about it! When he goes to the bathroom, who cleans up after him? When he wants to go out, who takes him out? When he needs a bath, who bathes him? When he is hungry, who feeds him; and who washes the dishes for him? And so on. This is all O.K., but on the other hand, shouldn't it also be O.K. when you want **him** to obey!

M. It's nonsense that in order to solve problems, you must catch the dog "in the act." In 90% of the cases, if handled correctly, the dog can be made aware of his misdeed, even if eight hours have passed since its occurrence. Therefore, a correction is applicable! In the case of the ten percenters, your correction should be **so correct** regarding the situation, that **aversion** has been implanted into your dog's brain. Thus the correction is valid in all respects!

N. Don't confuse your dog by letting him think that his name is a reprimand tone. **If you call his name, say something after it.** How many times have you seen and heard people with their dogs – the dog is in the trash, or sniffing some one's crotch, or acting like a wild hooligan – and their owner hollers, "PRINCE! PRINCE! PRINCE!" **Always** add a command after his name: "PRINCE – NO!", or "PRINCE – COME!" or "PRINCE – GO!"

O. If your dog happens to be the very dominant type – i.e. wants to drag you down the street every time he sees another dog, kitty-cat, or squirrel (I've seen more human broken bones and scrapes because of this); insists on getting into the trash; charges the front door every time you open it, etc. – **the time to solve the problem is before it happens!** Emphasize obedience in all aspects and at all times! Such as, when you command your dog to "Down!" or "Halt!" he should down or halt **"on a dime and get nine cents change!"** Any less than this **make a firm correction. Do not** wait until you are on the firing line!

P. Do you like to be pinned down in any way, shape or form to the point where you can not retreat? If someone goes to shake your hand and holds it for an unusually prolonged period of time, what is **your** tendency! To avoid temperament and psychological problems with your dog, **do not ever, for prolonged periods of time, physically pin down your dog or any part of him.** Always give him the option of retreat. Exceptions to this rule are noted in Lesson 107, Solving Misbehavior Situations, where the method of "Instantaneous Pinning and Release" is used in solving notorious misbehaviors.

Q. Have you ever heard it said that, **"The dog lives to please you!"** This is a comment that has been made many a time and written in many a book. **BUNK!** I'm here to tell you that the **true nature of the dog is that he is a very pushy animal.** He wants to please WHO...first? You betcha! And you...last...if at all! On the other hand, let's not be too hasty, he does want to please you, but only after you reverse the leadership pattern. **This is what training does – it reverses the leadership pattern.** Then he does want to please you, but only because there is a consequence – the **shock** factor, or a reward – the **love** factor!

R. In many instances the name you give your dog has an affect on his behavior and temperament. Many times we get calls for "Help! My dog is too aggressive. He wants to eat everybody!" I arrange for an evaluation meeting at their home. At the gate, I'm met by a Pit Bull, or a German Shepherd, or Cairn Terrier who wants to eat me alive! The people have to come out to the sidewalk to meet with me. One of my first questions is, "What's the dog's name?" The reply, "Oh, **Rocky!**" In another instance, "What's the dog's name?" The reply, "**Killer!**" And another, "**Ripper!**" **Is it any wonder why these dogs are aggressive?** Unbeknownst to the owner, people in general have been making moves on that dog since he was a puppy – moves that bring out...aggression! Can you picture it?

On the other hand, we have the person who complains, "My Doberman, Shepherd, Rottweiler, etc. is **not aggressive at all!**" "**What's the dog's name?**" I ask. "**Chrysanthemum!**" And another, "**Sweet Pea!**" And yet another, "**Lolly Pop!**"

What do you suppose the temperament of the Dalmatian named Dopey is like? Dopey belongs to a Mexican family...and family...and family...and family – grandparents, aunts, uncles, cousins, second cousins, etc. Can you imagine the chaos in that household! And who do you suppose is in the center of it all!

And what about Butkus, who is an 80 pound Chocolate Labrador Retriever. Butkus belongs to my neighbor, Anita. However, Anita doesn't refer to him as Butkus, as if that wasn't bad enough, she refers to him as, "The dog from hell." Can you imagine the damage that Butkus has done to Anita's home! And can you imagine the way Butkus greets company – have you ever seen how bowling pins scatter when one gets a strike!

Bobbie, owner of a notorious Doberman/Shepherd mix, shared with me that her television cable company serviceman has had "...to come to my home more times to replace wire and remote controls my dog has eaten that they now have a new code in their Service Manual: the code – Rascal!"

One of the looniest situations that I've ever walked into was this loony individual with three of the looniest, unruliest dogs I've ever seen. Their names Bing-

Bing, Bang-Bang, and...Dead Dog!

S. All human family members must be leaders over the dog. It is **certain** that if one is and others are not, **the dog will make it harder on the ones that are,** or he'll **find his nitch somewhere inbetween!**

T. Always remember that the **pack instinct is so ingrained** in the dog that regardless of how much or how well you train your dog, he will always reserve a little section in his brain that says, **"O.K., I'll perform, but mainly I do still own you!"**

U. That the dog forgets is nonsense! We receive calls from students that graduated six months to a year ago. "Dave, help! My dog's brain has turned to guacamole! He has forgotten everything!" When I meet with them, it has yet to fail that upon seeing me again, the dog turns shades of green, purple and white – I give **one** firm command and he does everything but salute!

V. For **all** misbehavior corrections, your command or your tone should be an emphatic "NO!" or "NO, NO, NO!" An example of this is: Dog jumps on you, as you swiftly (not to hurt, but **to shock**) drive your knee into his chest, your command is **not** "Down!" but – "NO!" You will find that soon your dog will immediately respond even to a passive "No!" before he reaches the contact point to whatever misbehavior.

W. A dog that reaches the age of four months or thereabouts and is still going to the bathroom in the house is **not** necessarily **not** housebroken. I've found that in the majority of the cases, the dog is only **marking** the territory. He is expressing the dominance that he has, not only over the household, itself, but the members within. This also holds true for a dog that marks every blade of grass, fire hydrant, telephone pole, etc. They **do not** have to do this. It is not a matter of needing to go to the bathroom. It is simply a matter of telling the world and all its members, **"King Tut** has been here, and is here to stay!" Or, simply, **"This is my turf!"** Can you imagine a guide dog for the blind **ever** doing this!

X. One of the questions which is most frequently asked by students is, "What is the hardest dog to train?" I slowly raise my eyes to meet theirs, "Well, you see, that is not the question. The question is, who are the hardest **people** to train, and the hardest people to train are those with little dogs." Why? The answer is simple. With bigger dogs, we may not hesitate to make a **firm** correction, but what do we normally do with little dogs? That's right, we spoil them...rotten!

Take for example the student who owns a one-year-old, five-year-old, or even a fifteen-year-old Yorkshire Terrier, that is still going to the bathroom in the middle of the living room, or in the master's bedroom, or better yet, their bed. I'm often asked, "Why?" My answer is, "If your dog was not a Yorkshire Terrier, but a Rottweiler, German Shepherd, Boxer, et al, would he still be going to the bathroom in the same areas? Think about it!"

Y. Many people believe that the dog should never cower down to the owner. To this I suggest: Do you think that we Marine Corps "boots," to one degree or another, don't go around with our tails between our legs during our initial training period? You betcha we do – every last one of us! The same applies to the dog! But does this continue indefinitely? Of course not! Not after we understand the rules. The same applies to the dog "in training."

Regardless of your nature, YOU must be the leader of the pack; there is no other way. If you have to train yourself to get tough, **do it!** If you have to join the U.S. Marine Corps, **do it!** There is no other way! A case in point is Sheri and her highly exuberant Labrador Retriever, Sam. Sheri is so easy going, the type of person that would not say "apple pie" if she had a mouthful.

Although we did make tremendous strides in the basic program and extra lessons that she had to have, at my last visit, I left her with the following **Get Tough Rx. diet**: Breakfast = 1/2 pound of nails; Lunch = 1/2 pound of thumb tacks; Dinner = 1/2 pound of each!

"**Z.**" When students first come to the school and we show them the lesson plan, many of them ask, "Dave, can we start with the Problem Solving lesson?" Though your tendency may be to do the same – **don't**! As I explain to the students, many people try to make corrections on their dog before they gain their leadership over him. **This doesn't follow.** If you can't tell your dog to sit and stay, and walk him on a leash halfway decently, how is he ever going to listen to you when you tell him not to jump on people or the furniture? **Stick to the lesson plan. Read this entire book from cover to cover. You'll be amazed at the end results! Don't cheat yourself...and your dog!**

TID-BITS TO PONDER AND REMEMBER

A. Please see A through Z above.

B. Please see A through Z above.

C. Please see A through Z above!!!

DR. JOSÉ MARIA GÓNZALEZ AHUAJE, D.D.S.
AND ROBO-COP
TIJUANA, BAJA CALIFORNIA NORTE, MEXICO

"Gracias! Gracias! Gracias!
Mi amigo, David, the best!"

DONNA JONES? BRANDON JONES? OR JOHN JONES?

THE LEADER OF THE PACK?

LESSON #102
THE PSYCHOLOGY OF TRAINING
THE TRUE NATURE BY WHICH A DOG THINKS AND LEARNS!

Many people complain about the sundry misbe-haviors of their dog.

● "My dog persists in going to the bathroom in the living room or the kid's room. Why?"

● "He jumps on everybody that comes in the house. Why?"

● "He eats the plants, charges the door every time we go to open it. The other day he ate the Bible. He won't leave the kitty-cat alone; and talk about leaving anything on the table or counter top. Forget it! Why? Why? Why?"

● "Take him for a walk, you say! Forget it! Forget it! Forget it!"

● "My dog attacked my wife, she had to have thirteen stitches on her face! Why? Why? Why?"

How often have we heard the question of who is smarter! You can bet your life that a dog **is** smart and he will find every way and try every maneuver to answer the question in the positive – **from his point of view, that is!**

Take just one of the many stories that I could tell you about Rev. Msgr. Raymond Kirk, a very gentle and genteel, 60-year-old priest at St. John of the Cross Catholic Church, Lemon Grove, California and his "so sweet" but highly challenging Dachshund, Leo. (See page 108).

Father Kirk and Leo went through the entire training course. For hopefully a "better response," he chose private lessons at their home. Leo responded to training excellently...**for me**...but...between Father Kirk and Leo, most of the time, I honestly can't tell you for sure who the leader of the pack is.

On this one occasion, when I attended Mass at 6:30 in the morning, there were very few people in church. I sat near one of the side doors, all was very still and quiet. All that could be heard were the prayers being said by the celebrating priest. Otherwise, you could have heard a pin drop. **When**...suddenly, on the side of the church I heard this patter and unmistakable metal collar sound. "Pitter-patter, jingle, jingle! Pitter-patter, jingle, jingle! Pitter-patter, jingle, jingle!" As I looked to the door, I saw Leo galloping by, trailing was his leash; and farther back, Father Kirk's voice in a hushed, exasperated tone, "Leo! Come! Heel! Leo! Heel! Come!" and Leo, as if he didn't know what to do, as if he was Rin Tin Tin, "blazing" the trail ahead! "Catch me...if you can!"

In my travels **throughout** my life, **throughout** the country, in umpteen places and umpteen circumstances – veterinarians' offices, parks, beaches, on freeways, in your neighborhood and mine – I have seen and experienced **all** these people...with **all** these dogs...with **all** these problems. **Why, when...it's...not...necessary! All these people being jerked around by their dogs. Enough is enough, is enough, is enough...is...enough!**

The best way that we can answer these questions and resolve these misbehaviors once and for all, is to **develop the ground rules** to "nip it in the bud!"; to "go to the root!" Here is where training begins and ends and it **can not** be any other way!

REV. MSGR. RAYMOND KIRK AND LEO

THE DOG IS A PACK ANIMAL!

The dog is basically an animal of the wild. He is a **pack** animal of the wild, a direct descendant of the wolf. Visualize a pack of dogs or a pack of wolves running in the wild. Use your imagination and picture the interaction of the pack's members. In my mind, the first one I see is...**THE LEADER; yes, the leader of the pack.** Secondly I see, clear in the back of the pack, a little runt. Because of his small-fry size, he is running twice as hard as everybody else, and because he is clear in the back, he is getting all the dust! Have you ever run in the back of a group? That's right, that's where you "get it all!" But, you know, time passes quickly for the little runt. Three months go by; five months go by; six, seven months go by; and what seems as suddenly, he is no longer a runt! He has most of his growth.

The "Runt" is now **bigger, stronger, meaner and tougher,** but he is still in the back and he is still running hard and he is still eating dust. However, now that he is bigger, stronger, meaner, and tougher he no longer likes being there...and he is thinking. What is he thinking? Well ...I believe we all know! So...**he** wants to be the leader! Who does he go to, to become the leader? And what does he do? Well...we know that eventually he has to get to the "top dog"...and...what does he do when he gets there? Nope...he doesn't fight him! Before a fight, there is always a **challenge.** Now, how do you suppose this challenge came into play? Could it be something like this:

Thinking that he is now big-fry size...and hot stuff...and mean...and strong...and tough, he just goes to the front of the pack and...**takes over!** And the leader, now somewhere in the back, says to the runt (in whatever manner they communicate), "Hey guy, get back to your place where you belong!" Now, what do you suppose the runt said? So...there is your challenge!

Let's examine this. Did the runt know what to do when he was told to do it? In the growing up process, how many times do you suppose he was "put in his place?" So, did he know what to do? **Yes, he knew exactly what to do, but he refused to do it! There is your challenge situation. He knew what to do, but he refused to do it!** Think about it. If you tell your dog to "Sit" and he **knows** how to "Sit," but refuses to do it, what is he doing to you? **You got it!** However, we want you to look at this as more than just a challenge. Because **it is** more than just a challenge. You know what it is – it's an obnoxious situation. You know what the dog is saying to you? That's right! He's telling you to "go fly a kite!"

And...look...as the runt was growing up, he kept straying from the pack and he would get lost in the canyons, the pack would come to a halt. **The little runt is lost again!** Who had to go get him? The leader. And...when he found him, he would carry him back. Where would he grab him? That's right! From the scruff of the neck. He would grab and shake him. Carry him back up to the pack. Shake him again and throw him down right in his place. If the little runt chose to go again, the leader would grab him again, shake and throw him back into his place, again, again, and again until he got it straight.

If you ever have to grab your dog, in a **corrective** situation, from any part of his body, where is the only place where it's appropriate and safe? That's right. The **scruff of the neck** and only the scruff. Don't let what happened in the following scenario happen to you.

A couple once called me to go to their home for an evaluation of their dog, a 9-month-old black Labrador Retriever, which they had just obtained from a friend who was being transferred overseas. I visited with them and they signed up for the program. Lessons were to start in a week. But the very next day, the wife called and cancelled. Why? The dog had been taken to the pound. Why? Because he had bitten their twelve-year-old son's face to the point of several stitches. Why? Because the dog was on the boy's bed and in trying to get him off, the boy pulled him off by the legs. The boy became a perfect target for the dog. **Again**

here is your challenge situation and why we should always use the scruff of the neck to grab the dog. In Lesson 101, "A Through Z Tid-Bits to Ponder, see tid-bit "P", page 96.

Let's go back to the wild, where the runt challenged the leader. Do you suppose that the leader **ever** allows the runt to tell him to "go fly a kite"?

After the challenge came **the fight.** Have you ever seen two dogs fight? Have you ever seen two dogs at hard play; very hard play? Picture them. Use your imagination. In both cases, have you ever noticed when they are chasing each other, how it appears as though they are traveling 100 miles per hour? They go zipping this way...and they go zipping that way; and as they are zipping by, they **grab** each other, **tumble** on the ground no matter what the surface – grass, gravel, cement, whatever. **They grab each other, tumble, roll and keep right on going as if nothing happened.** If they are coming around a bend and a picnic table is in the way, they'll **crash** into the picnic table. The table is perhaps knocked over, but the dogs, **they keep right on running**, as absolutely nothing has happened. A chair may be in the way...a wall may be in the way...**you** may be in the way; but, **the dogs, they keep right on trucking**—in spite of the **"brutality"** of their actions.

This description applies to any dog, whether it's a Labrador Retriever, Rottweiler, Golden Retriever, Pomeranian, Jack Russel Terrier, or French Poodle—within their own realm, their own power and strength—they all go through the same hard-knocks in a fight or hard-play situations. The related meaning of "within their own realm," is that all dogs learn through the same corrections, however, there are **degrees** regarding the forcefulness of the corrections. You would not use the same force on a Miniature Doberman Pincher as you would on a regular size Doberman Pincher, or Rottweiller, Labrador, or German Shepherd. **The correction must be commensurate with the type, size, and weight of the dog.**

Imagine for a moment, American football without the use of the tough protection, would the players ever live to tell the score! Imagine if you or I as humans were to imitate the dog's actions (their pirouettes) in a fight or at hard play, would **we** live to tell about it? It's doubtful. Think about it. We probably would not live to tell about it, **but the dog does. Within their own realm, their tenacity, their strength, and their power are unparalleled!**

What is the point I'm making? See if you can fill in the following very important blank: Unbeknown to most people, a dog, **generally** speaking, **can** take a licking and keep on _____!

PRINCE AND HONEY

Yes, a dog, generally speaking, can take a licking and keep on **ticking!** In other words, **generally speaking**, barring two-by-fours and baseball bats, it's very hard to hurt a dog. Because people don't know this and are afraid of hurting the "puppy," it is one of the main reasons why they end up with unruly dogs that literally dominate the household. Yet, dogs are not afraid to use their power against the human – **and...they...do!**

What is a dog made out of? Bone and very stout muscle.

It's not like you and I at all. On top of the muscle they have a tough hide. They can survive in areas you and I couldn't begin to survive. On top of the hide is the fur. With all this in mind, are we proposing that you should beat your dog into submission? Of course not! **Important to remember is that the dog does not learn by beating him in any way, shape or form!**

For example, I had a student who became a student only after his wife threatened divorce. Why? It seems that the husband came home one day and on arriving, found their Doberman/German Shepherd mix of seven months, had eaten the couch. And I mean **the entire couch.** He even scooted it out from the wall and ate the back of it! Was her husband upset? Would you be? On the spot, he took his belt off and severely beat the dog senseless. He threw him in the closet for two hours, brought him out and beat him again! What good did that do? Did his dog learn anything constructive from that experience? **A dog does not learn by beating him...ever...in any way, shape, or form.** This is very definitely a misconception on the part of many people.

However, another misconception is that, "You can never use your hand on the dog." Have you heard that one? I mean, people who are often aggressive and careless in their daily living, but **saintly** when it comes to their dog, will tell you, "Don't toucha my doggie."

The point here is, that in fact, you **can** use your hand. You are **not** going to hurt him. Remember what they are made out of and their own wild actions at play. **You are not going to hurt him!** You can use your hand. You can use your elbow. And...I mean right into the dog. You can use your knee. You can use your foot. And...I mean right into the dog. And...you can use the leash, right across his rear, or across **the bridge** of his muzzle (between the eyes and his nose), but **only if you use it properly**—in the way that dogs learn. Let us repeat again...you can use your hand, elbow, knee, foot and leash, but...**only if you do it properly, in the way that dogs learn.**

So what is properly? How **do** dogs learn? First, let's go back to the dogs' descendants—the wolf. The moral of that story is that the very same thing (and I mean the **very, very** same thing) that applies to wolves, applies to dogs. If you were to take your dog and turn him lose in the wild, he would revert to the wild, and he would run with a pack of dogs. Living here in San Diego, we don't have to go far to see a pack of dogs. Tijuana, Mexico is but thirty minutes away, and there you can see packs of dogs right in town. Believe me, they are dangerous!

So...what is the point? When you take the dog and

transfer him from the dog pack (that's where he came from), to the family pack, **to the dog there is no difference. A dog is a pack animal.** They need the relationship of the family members to live an adjusted life. **In many respects, they are no different than humans.** They have feelings. They have emotions. When owners neglect or are unaware of this, **that** is where the problems usually begin. However, the main point is that in this pack of yours (includes all family members and dogs), there must be a leader, **and who do you suppose is going to want to be the leader?** How do you suppose he is going to attempt that leadership? Remember the challenge situation. Who has to be the leader? Nope, it can not be just the older son. Nope, it can not be just Dad or Mom. **It has to be, and I mean it has to be, ALL the humans in the family.** Be it otherwise, and you can bet your life that the dog will find it's niche somewhere within the family.

How many homes have we been to where one of the family members will say to the dog, "Sit" and the dog immediately responds; "Sit" a hundred times in a row, and the dog immediately responds every time. Then another member comes in and says to the dog "Sit," "Sit," "Sit!" and the dog doesn't respond. Why doesn't he? Who has to be the leader? How are we going to establish leadership? **How do dogs learn?**

Let's get back to the story where the runt challenged the leader. What did the leader **really** say or do? He didn't say too much at all. He didn't do too much either. Not at first anyway. For you see, the leader, being older, wiser, meaner and stronger, did not get too excited. (**Never become excited when it comes to showing your leadership over the dog.** How many good leaders have been flighty, whimpy or hysterical?) The leader simply walked slowly and cautiously over to the runt, and in **ONE very firm maneuver** grabbed him by the scruff of the neck, turned him upside down, slammed and pinned him to the ground...or punched him right in the nose! In very definite tones demanded, **"You get back where you belong immediately. Do as I tell you to do!"** What do you suppose the runt did? You bet your life he did. With his ears straight back and tail between his legs, he went right to where he belonged.

In essence, didn't the leader have to **discipline** the runt to maintain order? Didn't he have to use some kind of **shocking** force? Wasn't this the only way in which he could maintain his superiority...his leadership? How many leader/subordinate situations have you seen where discipline did not enter into play? When was the last time you told your boss "where to go?" The ship, as a rule, has but one Captain, and **his word is law.** At the same time, remember that in good leadership situations, not only is one under the Captain's command, **he is also under his protection.**

So, what are we human pack members going to use to establish our leadership over the dog? What comprises a good leader? Guidance, compassion, understanding, instruction, and discipline. If you think about it, is not discipline really love? The bottom line is that we must have some form of **discipline,** which is equal to: **love!**.

What is discipline as it relates to the human vs. the dog? Discipline is comprised of three parts, and all three are very, very important.

THE THREE PARTS OF DISCIPLINE
LEADER VS. DOG

PART 1

The first part is the **disciplinary action itself** – the **shock factor.**

PART 2

The second part of discipline is always the love factor. Never, never, never, leave a dog after a disciplinary situation without coming back to the love factor. Not if you want your dog to grow up well adjusted and respectful of you. The love factor is what creates the good bond between you and your dog. Once the correction is over, **it is**

over. You must now come back with love. **I repeat, NEVER, NEVER, NEVER leave a dog after a disciplinary action without coming back to the love factor. However, don't overdo the love.** Some students will make a half decent correction only to nullify it through flowery love, "Puppy, it hurts me more than it hurts you!" Then hug, hug and...kiss, kiss and...cookie, cookie! I know more dogs that misbehave to get the hug, hug; kiss, kiss; and cookie, cookie. **Don't, don't overdo the love factor.** After disciplining, come back with a simple passive love tone, i.e., "Now **you be** a good puppy! **Be** a good puppy!" together with a loving pat on the head. Then **ignore** him for about ten minutes. Let him settle on his own.

PART 3

The third part to discipline is just that – ignore him! To the extent that he can remember or relate, **let him remember and relate** about what just took place. Don't **draw** him back to you; for then you would probably have to make yet another correction, and obviously, this would be...unfair!

But what about the **discipline?** As I beg all our students, I beg you: **be fair to your dog; be kind to your dog; and be a good leader.** If you are going to discipline him, **discipline him!** Get it over with! Don't be a ninny. Don't make a halfhearted, useless, ineffective and ridiculous correction, which only causes him **not to learn;** to come back with the same behavior, which only causes you to correct him again, and again, and again. It is better, kinder and more effective to correctly correct **once** than to have to correct for a lifetime!

Don't do like so many who...look, how many times have you seen people in the following situation with their dogs, or been guilty of it yourself: The dog is misbehaving – say, chewing the Bible, or a planter, edges of the carpet, the hose – and they say to the dog, "NO DOG, DON'T DO THAT, BAD, BAD, BAD, BAD, BAD! DON'T DO THAT!" And two minutes later...! Then they say to the dog over and over, "NO DOG!" "NO DOG!" "NO DOG!" Minutes, hours, days, weeks, months, year after year, they say to the dog, "NO, DOG!" "PLEEEEASE DOG! YOU ARE DRIVING ME CRAZY, DOG!" The years go by and then guess what? The puppy is no longer a cute, cuddly puppy. Now he's a **"moose – a no good moose!"**

When people reach that point, what do they do with their dogs? Some beat them. Some take them for a "ride in the country." Some may take them to the pound. In the end what do you suppose really happens to the dog? Is this fair to the dog? **Whose fault was it?**
I ask this of all our students and some will slowly lower

their heads and slowly raise them to meet my eyes and say, "It was the leader's fault, wasn't it?" "No, No," I respond, "it was the non-leader's fault!" Then I give a long pause and suggest, "I rest my case!" **Be kind to your dog. Be a good leader.** It is better to correctly correct once or twice than to correct ineffectively for a lifetime.

BEING A GOOD LEADER VS. THE PUBLIC

Being a good leader is one who does not pass on a correction because of the opinions of the general public. As a child will test you, so will your dog, and it probably won't be when you're alone with him. It'll be when company comes, when you meet a friend down the street, when you're taking him for a walk, or when the neighbors are "watching." When he tests you, when he challenges you, make a correction – **a correct correction.** Don't let people intimidate you out of a correct correction. It's your home and possessions that you don't want demolished. It is **you** who must answer to the animal law enforcement agencies to a neighbor's complaint, i.e., "Your dog barks constantly, all day long!" Chances are it's the same neighbor who cried foul in the "cruel" treatment of your dog. People don't know, neighbors don't know; they are not the ones that must answer for your dog, **you do!**

Picture the following situation: It was a bitter cold November day in Columbus, Ohio. Snow and ice was everywhere, and a chilling wind. I was standing in front of Moorehouse Fashion, a department store, and had just instructed a blind woman I was working with on how to go through very heavy glass doors. I explained how the dog would lead her to the door handle and the subsequent actions which she must perform. I was standing, arms crossed, about six feet away, observing my student on proper follow through; a maneuver which she and her dog would have to perform many, many times, without my guidance, after completion of training. Quietly, I continued to watch my students, blind master and dog, perform. Suddenly, a little old lady approached me, umbrella in hand and "drawn," as to strike me on the head.

"How dare you not help that poor blind woman!" The student was now fumbling, looking for the door handle. The little old lady persisted, "I ought to hit you. You have no compassion and no manners!" "I'm a trainer, ma'am," I tried to explain. "I don't care who you are!" she said sternly.

People do not know, neighbors do not know, and they are not responsible for your dog's actions, you are!

Furthermore, you can be sure, it's guaranteed, that if you let your dog win a little battle, he is going to make it tougher on you in another more important situation. You win the battles, all of them; you win the war! On the other hand, if he wins the battles...! **Be fair to your dog, be kind to your dog. If you must discipline him, discipline him, but do it correctly and consistently.**

CORRECTING YOUR DOG
THROUGH SHOCKLOVE

Shocklove is the term that I use to explain the disciplinary manner in which a dog basically learns. **The word "shock" means the element of surprise.** The shock (the discipline) must be firm, and I mean firm, sharp, and to the point. It must be unprolonged, **instantaneous**; and most importantly, if at all possible, the dog should not see it coming. Once again, discipline (shock) must be **firm, sharp, to the point, unprolonged, and most importantly, if possible, the dog should not see it coming.** The love factor, immediately following the shock, serves to reassure him of your continued support.

The bottom line, and I mean the very bottom line, of how a dog learns is through a **"shock"** factor – the element of surprise – followed by **love,** that reassures him. Shock the dog in the undesired situation and the dog will avoid the situation because he'll remember the shock that went with it.

Believe me, this combination, **shocklove**, is what **makes** the two of you:

A. The best of friends!
B. Leader – Subordinate!
C. A Better **C**ompanion **– A B**etter **C**anine!

And...this, I assure you, applies to practically all that you'll teach your dog, **especially** in misbehavior situations.

PRINCE, RAMBO AND HONEY
BETTER CANINES

The following are a few examples of **shocklove** corrections:

A. We were baby-sitting one of my student's big German Shepherd, Brandy. When traveling to clients' homes for training, I drive a station wagon and I take my three German Shepherds, Prince, Honey, and Rambo with me. Several times a day we perform the following routine: We come out of the building, go to the station wagon where Prince, Honey and Rambo always wait for me to open the back door and they jump in.

When Brandy came along, he wanted to change the routine. He would always get ahead of the pack and would not wait for the door to be opened for him. Instead he would leap through the back window – which was a beautiful sight indeed. We've taught many dogs to do this, but Brandy learned it on his own. However, Brandy would not only leap in, he would leap out. Therefore, I always had to tie him down.

For the majority of the time that we kept Brandy, he followed the same routine. Until one day when we went out of the building, he got ahead of the pack, went to the back of the car, and leaped through the window, but the window was closed! **Into it he crashed**, fell to the ground, looked up and shook his head – **never to do it again**. I even tried to get him to jump through the window, after I showed him that the window was open, "Look puppy, it's okay, it's okay, jump!" He looked at me as if to say, "No way, Jose. No way!"

The correction couldn't have been planned any better, even if we had been trying. Note that the correction was firm, sharp, to the point, instantaneous, and not prolonged, plus Brandy had no knowledge of how it came about. **A very true shock.**

B. While I was giving a lesson to Shirley and Bob in Point Loma, their 10-month-old Keeshond, Spikey, was chewing on the corner of their wicker coffee table – "chomp, chomp, rrrrip, chomp, chomp, rrrrip!" I slowly walked to the other side of the table, placed my foot on it, and in one swift move, drove the table into the dog, at the same time shouting the command, "NO!" The correction was firm, sharp, to the point, unprolonged, and as far as the puppy knew the table **"jumped"** out at him and **"bit"** his nose. How it came about he'll never know, but **he never went back to the table**.

C. I arrived at Pete and Corinne's home in Tierrasanta, California. They have three teenage children and a 95 pound, 2 1/2-year-old Yellow Labrador Retriever, named Barney. Pete, who, by the way, is a doctor, says to me, "Dave, it's like a zoo around here with this dog. You know, he has **us** trained to go out and eat every night. We can't sit at our dining room table for dinner anymore. The dog is not only under the table, but he is on top of the table, he's on top of us and he grabs the food! Put him outside, you say. Forget it! He bangs himself against the sliding glass door and the screen door, and barks and howls like someone is beating him to death."

That wasn't all, Pete continued describing Barney's misdeeds. "My wife refuses to go into the kitchen anymore. I don't know how many times this dog has knocked her down. Talk about going to the refrigerator, forget it! It's a **major** battle every time we go to the refrigerator. It's three o'clock in the morning, I can't sleep, so I come down stairs to get a glass of milk, and who do I have to fight with! Believe me Dave, it's every time and with everybody."

"Oh, come on, Pete! You mean to tell me that if I go to your refrigerator right now, your dog is going to do the same to me?" I asked this as the kids were snickering in the background. "Oh, come on, you guys, where's the kitchen, where's the refrigerator?" We headed for the kitchen. Guess who beat us there!

I had the family sit at the bar in the dining area. I walked to the refrigerator and opened it...**was I ever shocked!**

Barney was airborne as he crashed right into it!

I had seen this many times before, but never quite this bad. I am telling you that the shelves went flying one way, and the milk and everything else another. A good third of Barney's body was **in** the refrigerator. So what did I do? I didn't just close the refrigerator door. Remember this is a big dog and a big problem, and I don't go out to solve a problem and not succeed. With all my weight and strength, I shoved the door into Barney and held him in there for about five seconds, during which time he was obviously struggling to get out. Talk about rock 'n rolling, we made a mess, but he was making a mess anyhow! To Barney, it was a very long five seconds, if not...the bitter end!

I threw the door wide open, and as I did so, he **popped** out! As he ran, he looked back, and I hollered at him, "YOU WANT TO TRY THIS AGAIN?" I slammed the refrigerator door as I emphatically exclaimed, "THIS IS A NO!"

Barney was now huddling by the kids. I walked over to Barney and petted him with passive comforting words, "Now you **be** a good puppy!" We brought things back to normal and began the training session. I started the lecture on the psychology of how the dog learns. About twenty minutes later I said, "Pete, you know, I sure am thirsty, I sure could use a cold soda? Pete, you want a soda? Corinne,

you want one? O.K. everybody wants a soda. I'll get them!"
I went to the refrigerator, put my hand on the handle, slowly
opened it, and in the process, **Barney did scramble,** but
then he looked up at me, lowered his head, turned and
slowly tippy-toed out of the room. Never again did he try
his notorious refrigerator trick.

D. The classroom setting in our office is very much like
a normal living room. A couch sits against the wall, this is
where the students sit. In front of the couch, there's a wooden
coffee table. The dogs sit or lay between the table and the
couch at their master's feet. Thousands of dogs have lain
there – big dogs, cute dogs, wild dogs, skinny dogs, and fat
dogs. When giving the class lectures, I usually stand in front
of the table, opposite the side where the dogs are. If you
were to look at the edges and especially the corners of that
table on the dogs' side, you would find various nicks. Where
did they come from? You got it! And let me tell you, I
know that it is an old table, but it's my table; and I don't
want it chewed on anymore!

So what do you suppose I do the moment one of these
"moose" begin to chew on **my** table? Without hesitating, I
place my foot on the opposite side of the table and drive it
right into their mouth, as I sound off with, "NO! WHAT'S
THE MATTER WITH YOU!" And as I point to the table
where he started to chew, I emphatically command, "THIS

IS A NO!" I move the table back to it's original position and as I lower my voice and give him a pat on the head, "Now, you **be** a good boy!" How many dogs do you suppose have ever gone back to the table for a second try?

E. Kathie and her female poodle, Simone, live in a small apartment in La Mesa, California. In her small living room, in front of the television, Kathie has a very comfortable, good-looking chair and ottoman – the guest chair. But guess who took it over? Every time someone came near the chair, you got it, Simone would growl. Therefore, nobody could ever sit in that chair. So how did we correct this not-so-pleasant behavior with Simone? Knowing Simone's actions, I speedily headed for the chair, and on arrival, without hesitating and before she even had a chance to look up—I **sat** on her! And, purposely, I momentarily pinned her, where she had to struggle to get away. Simultaneously, I commanded, "YOU WATCH OUT! YOU GO LIE DOWN SOMEPLACE ELSE!" As I repeatedly hit the chair, I said, "THIS IS A NO! NO! NO! NOW YOU **BE** A GOOD GIRL. THIS IS A NO!" I got up from the chair, and as I patted her little head, I reassured her with, "Now you **be** a good girl!"

Subsequently, Kathie followed up with the correction by using the boomerangs. (The use of boomerangs is taught in Lesson 107, Solving Misbehavior Situations). If today you were to visit with Kathie and head for **any** chair Simone was in, what do you suppose Simone would do – you betcha' she would...**move!**

F. On occasion, **direct and obnoxious challenges** require direct action! Take for example the cases of Lucy (Hoffy) Hoffman and Mrs. Cabrillo.

1. Hoffy is a personal friend, a retired lady, living in La Mesa, California. She called for lessons with her Australian Shepherd, Lucky. Completely done in, she told me that, "Lucky is reaching the age of eight months, and is totally out of control!"

I arrived at Hoffy's for the first lesson. We're sitting in her living room, and during the entire psychology lesson, Lucky was obnoxiously jumping on the couch and on Hoffy. Over and over, Hoffy would push Lucky off; and over and over, Lucky persisted. Hoffy had scratches from Lucky all over her arms and legs. How many times have we seen this happen!

After about ten minutes of observing Lucky persist with this obnoxious behavior, I interrupted, "Hoffy, do you or do you not want to allow Lucky on the couch and all over you?" "Absolutely not!" Hoffy replied. "I don't want her on me or the furniture!" "Would you mind if I came over there and corrected Lucky for you?" "Please do!" Hoffy replied.

As I continued to talk, I casually walked over to the couch, where Lucky was all over Hoffy. In what appeared to be one continuous action, I **swiftly** grabbed Lucky by the scruff of the neck, shook her, and emphatically dropped her on the floor. At the same time, with the palm of my

**LUCY HOFFMAN "HOFFY" AND
HER AUSTRALIAN SHEPHERD, LUCKY**

hand, I began striking the couch. I picked up some of the throw pillows on the couch and threw them back on the couch, while sternly commanding, "DO YOU WANT TO GET UP HERE AGAIN? YOU WANT TO GET UP HERE ON HOFFY? THIS IS A NO! NO! NO! NO! NO!" Lucky ran under one of the end tables.

I ended the correction with my usual **love** tone, "Now you **be** a good girl. **Be** a good girl," while lightly patting her on the head. The entire maneuver was so dazzling to Lucky that Hoffy has often bragged, "Never again did Lucky get up on any of the furniture."

Lucky's training took place over four years ago. During those four years, I frequently visited Hoffy, and on arrival Lucky would wiggle, "smile," and anxiously await my acknowledgment of her greeting. As is the case with thousands of dogs that I've trained, the love affair between Lucky and myself couldn't be greater!

2. Mrs. Cabrillo, is an 83-year-old woman, weighing approximately 100 pounds, living in Vista, California with her approximately 70 pound, six-month-old Doberman Pinscher: "Help!" She and her daughter cried.

The match of Mrs. Cabrillo and Roxie was so unrealistic that even Little Red Riding Hood and Lobo would seem like lovers.

A thousand and one times in a row, I could command Roxie to sit, and a thousand and one times Roxie would respond **immediately**. Ten thousand and one times, Mrs. Cabrillo could command Roxie to sit, and ten thousand and one times, the command was not even heard by Roxie – **until,** I handed Mrs. Cabrillo a doubled-up second leash which I had her hold in her right hand and practice **striking** a trash can **with all her might**. Over and over we practiced, until I thought she was **ready.**

I had her go to Roxie with the following instructions:

a. Emphatically give your command to "SSSSIT!" Once!

b. If Roxie does not "sit," wait until her head turns away from you. No matter how long it takes. **Wait.**

c. When her head does turn, with all the strength that you can muster, pretend like her hind-end **is** the trash can.

I need not elaborate on Mrs. Cabrillo's hesitation to this action, but when zero hour came, she came through with flying colors. Did Roxie understand why she was **shocked?** You betcha' she did! After that, Mrs. Cabrillo had only to make the long "sss..." sound, and Roxie would **immediately** respond.

The Sit Command is one of the first commands by which you begin to gain your leadership. Therefore, as many of our students have used this maneuver, you may also have to do so with your dog. It's important to remember that the dog can never see the leash coming. He can never know that it was the leash that **shocked** him. Remember to use the **love** factor.

G. Melanie suggested that her German Shepherd, Kelsey, learned a lesson in trash on her own. "We have a tumbler-type lid on our trash can and she got her head caught in it – she has never gone back!"

Theresa believes that her Doberman Pinscher, Joe, also experienced a valuable lesson when he, "knocked the sliding glass door off it's track and it crashed into a million pieces—he's **never** jumped on the new one!"

"Z." As I was giving Martha Lopez of Chula Vista, California, the first lesson, her eight-month-old Dalmatian, Daisy, was between her legs and constantly licking them. Martha kept pushing her away with, "No, no, no." She had on shorts, and I noticed bruises on her legs. I stopped the lesson to say, "You know Martha, what you're experiencing is **dominant** behavior. Does Daisy have a **liquor** license?" Martha responded with, "She's not dominating me, she's tenderizing me, because then she **bites** me! She does this all the time...look!" As she showed me her bruises.

I had Martha place her hands so that she was holding the outside of her knees, and instructed her as follows. "When Daisy repeats that licking behavior, rapidly and shockingly close and open your legs giving them additional force with the strength of your arms and hands." Martha needed only to do this twice and Daisy backed right off and laid down for the remainder of the lecture.

NOTE: This last story explains the same method that we use to stop dogs from "crotch-sniffing" and "goosing-you" – some are notorious you know!

• If you are sitting, and a dog approaches to "crotch-sniff," do the same thing that Martha did with Daisy.

• If you are standing, and a dog approaches to "crotch-sniff," **shock** him with your knee. Do this by swiftly bringing up your right knee into his "chops" (mouth, muzzle). **See how many times he will come back!**

My life-long friend and business partner is Diana Dean, her "Daddy" is Harold Dean. When my German Shepherd, Prince, was about a year old, he experienced "the" crotch-sniff correction with Mr. Dean. Mr. Dean, who earlier in his life had raised Boxers, knew exactly what to do when Prince went to sniff him.

Mr. Dean was so smooth and nonchalant with his correction, he didn't even bat an eye. The correction he made with Prince was so impressive...so explosive...so clean, that Prince never approached him in that fashion again. Prince quickly gained respect for Mr. Dean, and so did I! I love the man and the way he carries himself – straight, sure, commanding, fair, and loving!

● If a dog approaches, or is in the act of goosing you, **swiftly, in a chopping manner**, bring your hand across your rear and into his muzzle (mouth, "chops"), or mule-kick him **right in the "chops!"** You get the idea.

TID-BITS TO PONDER AND REMEMBER

To summarize shocklove corrections, I suggest your thinking be as follows:

A. Regarding Brandy and the car window example. Who "bit" the dog? The window "bit" the dog. So what does the dog avoid?

B. Regarding the 10-month-old Keeshond chewing on the table. Who "bit" the dog? The table "bit" the dog. So what does the dog avoid?

C. Then there was Barney attacking the refrigerator. Who "bit" the dog? The refrigerator "bit" the dog. So what does the dog avoid?

D. Poodle Simone's possession of the guest chair also ended. Who "bit" the dog? The chair and the guest "bit" the dog. So what does the dog avoid?

E. In the case of Daisy, what "bit" the dog? Martha's knees and legs "bit" her, so what does the dog avoid?

"Z." Always remember the love factor.

IT'S MAGIC!

After explaining the above, I always show the students a little bit of magic.

A. I will make a coin disappear.

B. I will, in front of their eyes, change a cube from red to green.

"Z." I will, in front of their eyes, change a set of dice that show snake-eyes to another combination.

I do this to drive home the point that all magic is basically sleight of hand, meaning that to humans, the hand is quicker than the eye. This is even more so to the dog. Think about it. The dog doesn't see **at all** the way we do. Lesson 109, The Come Command, gives you a full explanation of a dog's vision.

To the dog the hand is quicker, so when he nips your hand or constantly licks them – backhand him. If you do it swiftly and explosively, **he will not see it coming**, but you cannot draw or call attention to the dog. The correction must be **shockingly explosive!** The hand **is** quicker, so is the elbow, the knee, the foot, the table, the chair, the refrigerator door, the front door, the screen door, etc. Remember the rule: Shock the dog in the undesired situation and the dog avoids the situation because of the **shock** that went with it. On the other hand, **do not forget** the **love** factor. SHOCKLOVE.

Any item that the dog "attacks" or is being obnoxious about can be used to SHOCKLOVE him. For example, if you are sweeping the porch, and the dog is in the way "attacking" **the broom**, what should shocklove the dog?

- And if you are lifting **weights?**
- And if you are **vacuuming** the floor?
- And if you have a pen in **hand** writing a check?
- And if he is under **foot** in the kitchen?
- And if he tries to run out the **gate?**
- And if you are **raking** leaves?
- And if you are **shoveling** snow?

You get the idea. Go for it! SHOCKLOVE!

STEVE WITH HIS
MINIATURE DOBERMAN PINSCHER, BAILEY

Although Bailey is a little tyke, by the end of the training, Steve
could have him do cartwheels. In spite of their great love affair,
Steve most definitely reversed the leadership pattern.

AT...."PLAY!"

RAMBO, HONEY AND SIMONE

THE "NOTORIOUS" DOG

When solving problems with your dog, most situations can be remedied with the shock factor and follow through with negative reinforcement. However, some dogs are very strong willed and will challenge you to the **nth** degree. In situations where the dog is **notorious**, there is but one remedy: **The Direct Approach**. See Lesson 107, The Direct Approach in Solving Misbehavior Situations.

As in the wild, when the challenger and the leader do battle, **you** must do battle, and at all costs, **you must win!** You win the battles, you win the war. He wins the battles, he wins the war. You can be sure that the nature of the dog is to accumulate a series of small victories over you, until such time that you have absolutely no control of him.

How many times have you seen people with their dogs say, "Dog, lie down." The dog raises its paw in the shake fashion, and what do they say, "Oh, how cute!" Cute perhaps, but he just won the battle. You can be sure that if you let him win one small battle here, and another one there, that when you go to a big battle, he is going to make it tough on you. Therefore, **YOU** win the battles. **All of them. YOU** win the war.

I have a brother-in-law James Siemer, who I admire, love and respect. I compare him only to my Dad – a man's man as when ships were made out of wood and men made out of steel. Still a youngster, Jimbo retired from the Columbus, Ohio Fire Department as a Fire Chief. Jim gave me this most effective and wise tid-bit, "Statistically many automobile accidents occur while one is backing up. To avoid this, **never, never, never** back-up more than what you have to." I use this knowledge every day in my driving. This same tid-bit is applicable in developing an effective shocklove leadership relation with your dog. Don't back away from your dog to the point where he wins the battle. Back-up, but just enough to where he **thinks** he is winning the battle and drops his guard; then come back with your correction in a very **explosive shocking way.**

Such as, if he jumps on you while you are sitting down, don't just lightly push him off, wait until he drops his guard and "thinks" he is winning the battle, then—"blast/shove" him off of you with a very commanding, "NO!" Believe me, he is not going to come back many more times—if at all! More than any other correction **at the office** under my guidance, this one prevails; as with any correction—**finality** should be your intent.

THE ULTIMATE CHALLENGE

The ultimate challenge is when a dog growls at or bites his master. The greatest sin of all is when a dog growls at or bites a child, regardless of the circumstances! In these cases **The Direct Approach** is in order. Show no mercy in your correction. You must get through to the dog your **total** disapproval.

If a 2 x 4 is the only thing near – use it. Use it right on the mouth or across the bridge of his nose. When I use the term 2 x 4, I'm obviously slightly exaggerating, and I use the term only for emphasis. On the other hand, I'm sure that you've read enough newspaper stories where not only would a 2 x 4 be warranted, but a .45 caliber pistol:

"BOY IS MAULED BY CRAZED DOG!"
"JOGGER IS ATTACKED BY TRIO OF DOGS!"
"MOTHER-IN-LAW IS 'EATEN' BY FAMILY DOG"

You are the one at the scene. **You** must make the judgment.

However, with **The Direct Approach** you must still use the element of surprise, and you must be **cautious**. Your correction should be so rapid-fire and so dazzling, that the dog has no idea "what-came-down." You can not go one-on-one against the dog and you **CAN NOT** beat him! You must still stick with the **shocklove** formula; **get it over with, and in a hurry.** There have been many a **man** (and here I use the term man as opposed to woman) who were bitten by their own dog. Why? Think about it.

As the mailman cautiously approached us, my uncle, Alfred, reassured him that his now loose Doberman Pinscher, Jay, would not bite. WITHOUT a wink or a smile, the mailman quickly shot back: "She's got teeth — don't she?"

ANY DOG has the propensity to bite; trained or untrained; Police Dog to Guide Dog for the Blind; Mastiff to Chihuahua; Rambo or Cookie, Killer or Sweetpea.

In "some" bite cases it can be determined that the bite occured due to a startling situation for the dog; some, wrong handling; others, provocation and/or irresponsibility or just plain stupidity from one of our more "illustrious and highly educated" human ignoramusses; but, in many other cases WE JUST DON'T KNOW WHY?!

We do not know for sure what death and the hereafter is like, I have yet to hear the interview from the mouth of a human that came back to tell us. By the same token, I have yet to hear the interview FROM A DOG'S MOUTH as to why he bit.

The same as humans have mood swings, so do dogs. When was the last time a "human" growled at and/or "bit"

you—AND YOU HAD NO IDEA WHY? ANY DOG has the propensity to bite and in many cases, WE JUST DON'T KNOW WHY!

Dogs sometimes misinterpret as questionable and/or aggressive the overly cautious or overly exhuberant/friendly approaches from a human.

When dealing with any dog, common sense and respect are always THE ORDER OF THE DAY. Your approach towards the dog should always be as "normal" as it can be, nonchalant, friendly, and cautious. With "questionable" dogs you will find it to be A BETTER MEETING if you let the dog approach you first. ANY DOG has the propensity to bite and in many cases, WE JUST DON'T KNOW WHY!

With all this in mind, we can begin to gain our leadership. Gaining our leadership begins with obedience training, and obedience training begins with the proper use of the equipment.

TID-BITS TO PONDER AND REMEMBER

To review the nature of **How a Dog Learns** remember:

A. They are very definitely pack animals.

B. In the pack, there must be a leader.

C. The leader must be patient, strong, but fair. When

dealing with your dog, carry yourself in a **commanding way; never be** flighty, whimpy, or hysterical!

D. Discipline must be firm, sharp, to the point, unprolonged, and most important, if at all possible, the dog **must not** see it coming.

E. The last part of discipline is the love factor. When the correction is over, **it is over**. You must return to love!.

F. The very, very, last part of a correction is to ignore the dog for a few minutes. To the extent that they can remember or relate, let them remember or relate the correction that transpired.

"Z." The bottom line of solving misbehavior situations is the **shock** factor; the **element of surprise. Shock** the dog in the undesired situation and the dog learns to avoid the situation, because they remember the **shock** that went with it. Do not forget the **love** factor! **SHOCKLOVE.**

Shock does not mean **hurt!** In many cases just the "quickness" of movement will shock — you **do not** always have to ... **connect!**

LESSON #103
BASIC EQUIPMENT
PROPER USE OF THE TRAINING COLLAR AND THE LEASH

THE TRAINING COLLAR

The training collar should be a slip-chain type. Heavy duty links are preferred, but this depends on the size and weight of your dog. Usually a dog under 15 pounds should have a light weight, small link collar. All others, a heavy weight, large link collar.

Thinking that it's **kinder** to the dog, the tendency of many people is to use a thin, light weight collar. Remember when we were kids and tied a string around our arm. Remember how it had a tendency to cut? Or picture a rubber band around your arm, it does the same thing.

Now picture that light weight, small link collar on your large dog's neck and multiply the **unkindness** by the number of times that it will tighten or the jerks that you'll give. If your dog (size and weight permitting) can handle a **large link collar** – let it be so!

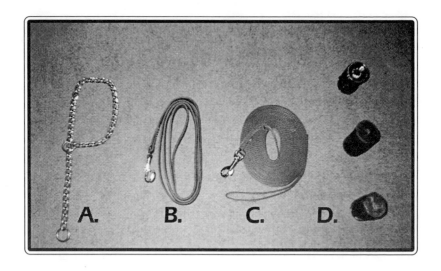

**THIS IS ALL THE EQUIPMENT YOU NEED FOR
BASIC TRAINING.**

A. Slip-chain collar. Note that it looks like the letter "p" when properly threaded and placed on your dog as you are facing him.

B. Standard 6' leather leash.

C. 30' lunge line – webbed long leash. This is used in place of the standard 6 foot leather leash when more control at a distance is needed.

D. The boomerangs. Three 6 oz. tin cans with 15 washers, pennies, or small stones in them.

This collar is commonly known in the dog world as **the choke collar**, but unfortunately this is a misnomer. We learned in Lesson 102 that a dog basically learns through a **shock** factor, and not a choke situation. **So the training collar is not a choke collar.** With the exception of a very aggressive situation, dogs do not learn anything by choking them.

The slip-chain collar, if anything, is a **shock** collar. Unfortunately many years ago, somebody along the way, got this whole situation, as I like to say, "corn-fused." It caught on to the point that today trainers call them chokers; groomers call them chokers; and pet stores sell them as chokers. If this is the case, when the lay person gets hold of them, how are they going to use them?

How many times have you seen (or maybe been guilty of it yourself) what I like to call, dogs walking their people! The dog is pulling with all his might and the master is responding in kind. Down the street they go, the master commanding, "Heel! Heel! Heel!" The dog responding, "Choke! Choke! Choke!" I've seen this happen to more dogs, all sizes and all types. By the end of the walk, you look at their tongues, and you'd think they were all Chow Chows! Have you ever seen the tongue of a Chow Chow? They are black or purple.

Carol demonstrates the correct threading of the training collar. As you face this example, the collar on her right arm forms the letter "p"— this is the correct way — not the letter "q" as demonstrated on her left arm. See point "B" on the next page.

THE PROPER USE OF THE TRAINING COLLAR

There is a **right** and **wrong** way of putting on and using the training collar. To make certain that it's on correctly, follow the instructions below.

A. Thread the collar through one of the rings; they are both the same.

B. With your **left** hand, hold the collar so that it forms the letter "p" (not "q" when reversed.) As the years have gone by, we have found that many people get their "p's" and "q's" confused! Make sure that it is a "p" as in **pet, puppy,** or the proper way.

C. Put your **right** hand through the "p" and open it all the way. It should now look like a bracelet on your **right** wrist.

D. Go to the dog, face him, and as you are facing him, with your **right** hand, grab his muzzle (mouth).

E. With your **left** hand, transfer the collar to his neck. **Because dogs do not like to be pinned down, this maneuver should be done swiftly. Don't dilly-dally!**

Note the correct "p" placement of the training collar on Poo Bear by Marilyn Tenbrook.

F. Many dogs run at the sight of a training collar. The collar was put on the dog when he was too young. The dog is either tired of being choked, or the master, while fumbling through the experience of putting it on, created a traumatic experience for the dog. The maneuver should be practiced first with a family member, using this person's right hand and arm as the dog's muzzle.

G. The **proper fit** is where it slips over the dog's head snug but comfortably; a wedge should not be required to put it on and off. In determining the right fit, there should be a 2 1/2 to 3 inches of play when the collar is tightened; or two fingers in vertical order, should easily slip between the dog's neck and collar.

H. A question that is often asked, "Should the collar be left on the dog at all times?" In the dog world there are many different opinions. My opinion is, that for toy-type dogs, use it only for training purposes. However, if the collar fits properly and good judgment is used, there isn't a reason why the training collar can not be worn 100% of the time. Especially if he is a large dog. I have yet to know the guide dog, hearing dog, or any of my personal dogs that didn't wear a slip chain collar 100% of the time.

"Z." **Never** tie a dog next to an obstacle that he can jump, **especially** if he is wearing a slip chain collar. Do not leave the collar on if the dog is kept in an area with much foliage, wire fencing, or areas where the collar can easily become hooked. This is particularly important at the beginning of training. With this in mind, allow the dog to become accustomed to it using the following small steps:

1. First, let him wear it for five minutes, then fifteen minutes, a half-hour, and so on, up to two hours.

This is the proper way of holding the leash
at the heel position.

2. After this, attach the leash, and **under your supervision**, let him drag the leash. Do this for two or three days, first for five minutes, then fifteen minutes, and so on.

3. After the dog gets used to dragging the leash, pick up the end of the leash and **follow wherever he goes**. Again do this for two or three days, first for five minutes, then fifteen minutes, and so on.

4. Do not let the leash tighten. **Little by little** you can now start maneuvering the dog using the leash by giving small **jerks**, and going the way **you** want to.

5. A **jerk** on the leash is one that in **split-second** order, tightens and immediately loosens. It provides a shock to the dog. A **shock** that he'll learn to avoid by not straying any farther than the length of the leash which his master has allowed.

6. When introducing the training collar to your dog, don't create a traumatic experience. One step at a time will provide **miraculous results!** This applies to all the training.

THE LEASH

The leash is simply an **extension of the collar**. It should preferably be made of high-quality leather,

and be 6' long. The width depends on your dog's size; dogs
15 pounds and under – 1/4"; 15 pounds to 65 pounds –
5/8"; 65 pounds to 95 pounds – 3/4"; and over 95 pounds –
3/4" to 1". Few dogs should require a leash which is wider
than 5/8". Any wider than this will only hinder your handling the leash.

For the lay person, a good leather leash can, if well cared
for, last a lifetime. Personally, I've had leashes that lasted
twenty years, and this is with daily use. To care for your
leash, periodically, rub into it a good salve or oil (linseed or
even baby oil). This will make it pliable and easy for you to
handle.

As I said, the leash is simply an extension of the collar,
and it should **never be allowed to tighten between you
and your dog. Your dog can't tighten it, but neither can
you.** Should the dog, at any time, start to take out slack
you've given, consider it a challenge and immediately give a
jerk. The jerk should be **swift** and **to the point.** It's better to
correctly jerk once or twice, than to have to jerk a lifetime.
In the proper use of the collar and leash, the idea is to keep
them **loose at all times.** This resembles **off-leash** conditions and control. Isn't this what we're trying to accomplish?

PROPER USE OF THE LEASH

A. At the **heel** position, the **handle** of the leash is in your **right** hand, your **left** hand is somewhere **center** of the leash. This depends on your height and your dog's size. In any event, be sure that **between** your left hand and the dog's neck the leash forms a "U." The leash must **always** form a "U" in order to remain loose.

B. The idea behind **all** training is not to force, control or try to physically get the dog to perform. The idea is to teach the dog to **control himself** and perform on his own recognizance, hence the keeping of the leash loose at all times. **Period.**

C. Many of the students have the tendency to hold the leash too short between their left hand and the dog's neck. To be certain they avoid this error, I always tie a knot on their leash at the correct left hand place. To make sure that you are holding the leash properly, do the following:

1. Stand at the heel position. The dog is on your **left,** one foot away. Its front paws in line with the back of your heels. This is precisely what "heel" means – whether you are standing or walking.

2. Place your **right** hand on the handle of the leash.

3. Place your **left** hand on the center of the leash. The leash is now forming a "U" between your left hand and the dog's neck.

4. As you're holding the leash—your arms are hanging normally along the side of your body—**shorten** or **lengthen** the leash between your left hand and the dog so the **bottom** of the "U" is in line with the **bottom** of the dog's chest.

5. After making the proper adjustments, tie a knot at the point where your **left** hand is.

6. Make it a habit to always grab the knot with your left hand, and you'll never go wrong! See example on page number 156 for the correct way of holding the leash at the heel position.

7. Three extremely important thoughts to remember in the proper use of the leash and the shock collar are:

● Never tie yourself to the dog with the leash. Many that have, have experienced cuts, scrapes, and broken bones when their dog bolted. The loop at the handle of the leash is strictly for hanging the leash. Never put your thumb, hand, or wrist through it. In a push-comes-to-shove situation, let the dog go. Do **not** put yourself in harm's-way.

EDITH AND MORENA DEMONSTRATE
THE PROPER JERK

With both hands on the handle of the leash, spin your body, face the dog...

...and jerk!

See point "Z" page 163

• The jerk on the leash is one of the most effective handling techniques and one of the most used in the training of your dog. Give a jerk when the dog starts to "mark" the territory (couch, chair, fire hydrant, end of counter, table, telephone pole, etc.). Give a jerk when the dog jumps on a person or furniture, or if he starts to chew the corner of the table, chair, hose, and/or plant. The same applies if the dog tries to run into the street; growls or barks at a non-threatening situation; or chases the kitty-cat, etc.

• However, the jerk, the "proper" jerk, is a technique which most students have difficulty with. In many cases their jerks are **too light**, causing them to give them way **too many times**; time and time, and time again. In most situations, the students are not jerking at all, but pulling or **jerk-pulling**.

D. The "Proper" Jerk

There is a definite difference between pulling, jerk-pulling and properly jerking the leash. When you pull on the leash, you're causing the shock collar to tighten and **not** immediately release. You're actually **choking** the dog. The period of time during which the leash is tight (doesn't have slack in it) lasts from two seconds to an indefinite period of time. It usually resembles a tug-of-war situation. The same applies to the jerk-pull, except the period of time during which the leash is tight is about three or four seconds. When using the **correct jerk,** the action on the leash is so swift that it does not create a choke situation. It's done so quickly, that the period during which the leash is tight lasts just a fraction of a second, and thus produces a **shock.**

E. A good way to learn how to give a proper jerk is to attach the leash to a cyclone fence; vary the distance you stand from the fence; keep the leash loose; and with your left, right or both hands on the leash jerk, jerk, jerk! Make the fence reverberate. The more you can make the fence reverberate, the more you'll know that your jerks are becoming proper. For you fishermen and women, the action of the jerk should resemble the setting of the hook on the fish after you've snagged it.

F. Preferably the jerk should be given in the **opposite direction** from where the dog's incorrect behavior is occurring. For example, if the dog tries to get ahead of you – jerk to the rear; if the dog pulls to the left – jerk to the right; the dog is lunging and barking – jerk in the opposite direction he is lunging and barking.

"Z." If your dog tangles the leash around your legs, untangle yourself by automatically spinning in the opposite direction. Keep the dog in front of you and **both hands** on the handle of the leash. You're now in a position to give a swift jerk. If you need to, for a greater effect, throw your body weight backwards as you jerk. This also applies to more formidable and extra challenging dogs. See examples on pages 161, 170, 171, 174 and 175.

TID-BITS TO PONDER AND REMEMBER

A. The training collar is designed to **shock, not to choke,** the dog.

B. Remember your "p's" and "q's" regarding the proper way of putting on the **shock** collar.

C. The collar and leash **should never** be allowed to tighten between you and your dog.

"Z." The **proper** jerk on the leash and collar **shocks** the dog and **immediately** releases.

The purpose of obedience and behavior training is reversal of patterns of who owns who — making you The leader of the Pack! Read this book from cover to cover!

Happiness is... **A Better Canine!**

THE PERFECT HEEL

Margaret Adams and Sam

LESSON #104
THE HEEL COMMAND
BEGINNING TECHNIQUES

The story has it that Sally and Jane met for breakfast.

Sally – "I thought your husband was going to join us this morning."

Jane – "Oh no, he's at the doctor having his tennis-elbow treated."

Sally – "I didn't know he played tennis."

Jane – "He doesn't. He got it walking the dog!"

How many times have you seen what I like to call "dogs walking their people." How many times have we received the same call, "My dog dragged me down the street. I broke my wrist, my nose; and my knees are all scarred."

How many times have I received messages on my voice mail such as, "There is **no way** that we can walk our dog. Please call as soon as possible, because he is impossible!"

The definition of the **"Heel"** command is that the dog

must always stand or walk on your **left** side, with his front paws directly in line with the back of **your** heels. This is the ideal or **perfect** position. However, he may be allowed to walk a foot or so in back of you, but **never** in front of you, which is, after all, where his tendencies will be. Remember, **the leader of the pack.**

As a general rule, all trained dogs walk on the **left** side of their master. The reason is simple: A trained dog is one that is **basically** and **naturally**, out of the way, and they are more out of the way on the left side because we live in a predominantly right-handed world. With our right hand, we shake hands, open car doors, open front doors, carry packages, etc.

Sniffing or marking every blade of grass, telephone pole or fire hydrant that comes along is **not** allowed. Many students believed that this was part of the dog's nature; that you had to allow them to sniff and mark their territory. **You don't!** A dog that does this is one that thinks he is very dominant over his "non-master" and every territory he encounters. **"This is my turf!"** Can you just imagine a guide dog for the blind doing this! If your dog does this, **break him of it. Jerk** every time he does it. If he persists, **shockingly** put the upper, soft part of your foot (this can be done with your shoes on) right into his muzzle; but, again, **use judgment,** and don't forget the **LOVE!** See page 182.

Before beginning training – remember the following:

A. The right age – you don't want to traumatize the dog.

B. The right leash.

C. The right collar; with the right fit and the right usage.

"**Z.**" By now the dog should already be used to the leash and the collar. If not, see Lesson 103.

ALFRED DRUEBBER AND RUSTY

"Prior to this training, I could not even begin to walk Rusty.
He knocked me down, but no more."

ALFRED DRUEBBER AND RUSTY

The proper position and hold of the leash,
at the very beginning of training.

TRAINING

A. Place the collar and the leash on the dog. **With both hands, hold onto the end of the leash.** The hold should resemble that of holding a baseball bat, keeping both of your hands together – even a 1/4" separation would cause you to lose half of your power when giving a jerk. Keep the dog's body **in front** of you at all times. If he tries to circle you, simply spin your body so as to keep the dog in front of you. At all times keep him in front of you. Allowing him to circle you signifies dominant behavior – as in the wild. **Do not allow it.**

Should the dog begin to tighten the leash, extend both arms out, so as to create slack on the leash, and jerk backwards, towards you. If your dog is large and formidable, throw your body weight into the jerk.

At all times you must keep the leash loose and off the ground, and so must your dog. From you to the dog, it must always look like the letter "U" or thereabouts. If the dog, at any time, begins to bolt or aggressively fight the leash, hold your ground and jerk him back.

If your dog is the type that fights the leash in a shy or scared way, **do not** hold your ground, but keep the leash loose by going with him. Every time he stops, give him lots of assurance before you proceed.

If your dog is the type that **emotionally, totally and completely** loses it every time you put the collar and leash on, I strongly suggest that you seek professional help, but be sure that it is **professional.** Your veterinarian is a good reference for a professional trainer.

B. After the dog settles down, head outside. When you get to your door or gate, open it wide and commence to walk through it. Should your dog bolt, jerk him back and try again. At this time, your dog may be anywhere around or in front of you, preferably he's on your left. The only thing you want him to do **at this time** is to walk through that door or gate, without tightening the leash – to walk through, **like a gentleman or a lady!**

C. Proceed to walk around the area, maintaining the leash as explained. At the beginning, set the course you travel, lightly. In other words, **go with him** much of the time, **even if he is in front of you.** Do not give too many jerks, but quickly begin to gain command over him by having him walk **only** the course that you have set. At this time the only thing that **you don't** want the dog to do is to tighten the leash while you're walking.

D. After about three days, you should be able to walk the course **you set** without having to give too many jerks. At this time have the dog stand still as **you align** yourself to

A.

B.

C.

A. At the beginning, keep the dog in front of you at all times. Don't let him circle you.

B. As the dog begins to tighten the leash, extend your arms to create slack on the leash and the collar...

C. ...and jerk!

him at the heel position. **Note – I said you align yourself to him.** In the beginning, you always align yourself to him. Because this is new to the dog, it would be unfair to pull him to you. If you did, his tendency would be to pull in the opposite direction. As time and training go by, he will naturally fall into the right place. If he moves after you are in position, or when you are trying to align yourself to him, give a firm jerk, as you command, "NO!" and try again. But remember that only **one jerk is allowed for every time he moves.** If you were to give more than one, the second and subsequent jerks would no longer be shocks but aggressive behavior on your part and, therefore, **unfair.**

E. You are now at the heel position. Be sure you're holding the leash properly (see Lesson 103, page 156) and give the command "HEEL!" or "PRINCE, HEEL!" Use the name of your dog only if you need to get his attention, otherwise, don't. Commence walking with your **left foot.** This will become his signal to walk at heel. Later you don't have to use the verbal command, but simply lead off with your left foot—he will follow.

If your dog refuses to move, you keep going. In other words, drag him as you give encouraging tones, "Come-on, come-on," and gestures, i.e. pat your left leg; but **do not jerk him.** This is the only exception to the tightening of the leash between you and your dog. **If he freezes or balks,** you keep going. **Do not stop!** For it is **he** that is tightening the leash. You'll find in most cases he will quickly relinquish the idea of lagging and catch up to you. Should your dog be one that totally freaks-out, again, consult a professional trainer.

As you are walking at heel, the moment that the dog attempts to get ahead or to either side of you, with your left hand and arm, swiftly jerk, as you command, "NO!" or "HEEL!" or "NO – HEEL!"

"Z." When you stop, **stop abruptly,** as you heavily shuffle your feet in a shocking way. This shuffle is a definite attention-getter and will become his signal to stop. Later you don't have to shuffle (you'll know when), simply stop normally and he'll respond in kind. If he tries to get ahead when you stop, jerk as you command "NO!" After stopping, if you need to, align yourself to him and try again.

A maneuver that is helpful in keeping the dog in position, whether walking or stopping, is to walk beside or **stop by left obstacles,** i.e. walls, fences, cars, telephone poles, etc. In other words, **crowd him** against these obstacles. We use these same techniques to correct dogs that have tendencies of 1) turning to the left, or 2) turning in front of you every time you stop.

During the entire process do not forget your praise of him if he is performing well. Such as, when you're walking, give encouraging remarks, "Good Boy! Good Boy!" and gestures such as patting your left leg as you walk. On the other hand, don't overdo it.

If you are practicing with your dog **at least twenty minutes per day, every other day,** two weeks should go by before advancing to the next lesson, The Heel Command (Advanced Techniques); The Sit and the Automatic Sit.

TID-BITS TO PONDER AND REMEMBER

A. Before beginning to train your dog, remember the following:
- The right age.
- The right leash.
- The right collar.
- The right use of the equipment.

B. Before attempting **formal** walks at the heel position, be certain that you are first able to walk any course, as explained in paragraph C, and with both hands at the end of the leash resembling a baseball bat hold. See page 171.

C. Remember to shuffle when you stop.

D. We encourage you to use loving remarks and gestures.

"Z." Do not create additional trauma for your dog if he tends at any time, in a shy or scared manner, to lose it. Consult a professional trainer.

THE BASEBALL BAT HOLD

Christina Gminski and Jake. The "baseball bat" hold is very important at the very beginning of training.

AUTOMATIC SIT AT HEEL

Courtney and Zoe

Notice the "looseness" of the leash and its "proper" hold.

LESSON #105
THE HEEL COMMAND – ADVANCED TECHNIQUES
THE SIT AND THE AUTOMATIC SIT

For two weeks you've been practicing the Heel Command, and if you fall within the norm of 98% of the students, you and your dog **are** doing a lot better! However, periodically your dog still tries to get ahead of you, and when he does you **jerk.** In some cases you **jerk** and **jerk** until your hand and shoulder hurt.

Why – after all this time is your dog periodically still trying to get ahead of you? The answer, regardless of the circumstances, i.e. another dog passes by, a kitty-cat appears, or a leaf falls off a tree, is simple. He is not yet convinced that **you** are **The Leader.** So...down the street you go...and Jerk! and Jerk! and Jerk!

The news, **starting this lesson,** is that you are to **avoid** the jerk at heel. Avoid! Avoid! Avoid! Don't get me wrong – use the jerk technique, **but only if it's absolutely and totally necessary.** Otherwise – Avoid! Avoid! Avoid! **Why**

182   THE ABC'S OF DOG TRAINING ...AND YOU!

you may wonder! First of all, if you were to continue giving the jerk, you would never totally control the dog off the leash. He would always expect that jerk for control. Secondly, in most cases, the jerk by this time just doesn't mean anything to the dog.

Again you may wonder, "If we can't control him with the jerk, how are we going to control him?" Starting today, we're going to control him through what we call **direct, personal, shocking maneuvers,** as is done out in the wild directly from the leader of the pack. To help you visualize these maneuvers, picture this guide-dog situation. A blind person is walking down the street with their guide dog. They arrive at the curb. What does the guide dog do? What would you want him to do if you were blind? Of course the dog stops! If he didn't stop, what would be the first thing to happen to the blind person? He would trip, and from there on...heaven only knows!

How do you suppose we trainers taught that dog to stop for that curb and every other hundreds of thousands of curbs that he will encounter? We did it through **personal shocking maneuvers.** Exactly what did we do? When we train a guide-dog, we're essentially pretending to be blind. So if the dog that I'm training fails to stop for a given curb, **what do I do? I trip!** Plus I exaggerate the fall or stumble, making certain the entire maneuver is **shockingly** uncomfortable for the dog. I point to the curb and then reassure him with a little love. I then take him back a few paces and again head toward that same curb. What do you suppose the dog will do this time? You can be certain it doesn't take many times for the dog to experience these **shocking maneuvers** before he stops at the curb – **every time**. To reinforce the behavior, every time he does stop, we connect with the **love factor**. "Good boy ! Good boy!" combined with an equally **loving** pat on the head.

In your training, you're not going to fall over your dog, but you are going to do something similar.

Should your dog be too formidable, too powerful, or too crazy FOR YOU to handle and/or do shocking maneuvers on, do not put yourself in harms way; simply outwit him: FORGET THE PERFECT HEEL and walk him ONLY using the "base-ball bat hold" on the leash, AND CORRECT TECHNIQUES as explained. This is what will give YOU the most power and control over him. See Pages 170 and 171. Preferably use a 4 foot leash.

DOG OR ANTEATER?

Turn and shockingly tap his nose with the upper part of your foot. One shocking tap is equal to 100 jerks!

Notice the "looseness" of the leash and its "proper" hold.

TRAINING

A. Give the command to "Heel!" Be sure to keep your leash very loose. **The moment** that your dog begins to get ahead of you, even by a nose, you're going to do an **abrupt, shocking**—without stopping—90 degree turn to the **left**. If you ram him or step on him, don't worry about it, **keep moving** in the direction that you just turned. Do this every time he tries to get ahead of you. During practice, do a series of left turns; in essence, **walk a square** about nine to ten feet per side.

In this maneuver, remember two points:

1. The maneuver must be made as if it was the dog's fault – **he** is in the way.

2. The maneuver must be done in a **shocking way** – **not a hurting way**.

I call this to your attention because of one student's cruelty that comes to mind. He made his left turn and in a gunning, premeditated and very forceful way, kneed his Golden Retriever in the rib cage. A maneuver which I obviously immediately brought to a halt. **These maneuvers are not meant to hurt...they are meant to shock.**

B. To emphasize his staying in back of you, you're periodically going to do **left-about turns**. Not U-turns, but turns that actually take you back in precisely the same direction where you were coming from. If the dog is in the way, **run him over. Do not** go around him. Make it **uncomfortable** for him.

When doing this maneuver, many students end up tangled in the leash. To avoid this, make sure that when you go into the dog you **go into him from his left** and not his right side. Should you become tangled, take advantage of it, and as best you can, untangle yourself, but in the process...**keep moving!** Make the whole process appear to be your dog's fault and **very shocking!** It's up to the dog to yield to you, recognizing you as the leader of the pack.

C. Should your dog manage to take the lead away from you, getting too far ahead of you to the point where you can not do a 90 degree left or left-about, simply do a 90 degree right or right-about. You'll find that this will immediately take the lead away from him.

D. Should your dog be one that is notorious about taking the lead after you do a right-about, then **immediately following** this right-about do a left-about. In other words, "cut him off at the pass!"

You may then continue evasive zig-zag maneuvers. Picture war movies at sea, where John Wayne commands, "Evasive maneuvers, full speed ahead!" And the ship travels in a zig-zag pattern. The same as that ship, make many of your training walks in a zig-zag pattern (even if you look like you had one too many for the road) and every time your dog gets in the way, **bump-shock him!**

E. Towards the second week of training this lesson, you should be combining your different shocking maneuvers. A maneuver that caps all of them is to do 8' to 10' circles. Circle left – when you reach the beginning, do a left-about and circle right. Complete the maneuver by doing figure eights. If at any point the dog gets in the way, with your knee or foot, **shockingly** ram him! The two most important maneuvers are the 90 degree lefts and the left-about turns – **make...the...dog...yield...to you!**

By doing these mixed shocking maneuvers, you'll find that:

1. Your dog begins to realize that the only safe place to be is to your left and directly in back of you.

2. He'll pay attention to you first and everything else second – which is, after all, **the way it should be.** By doing this, **you** will set the pace – **not the dog.** Can you imagine a guide-dog, at any time, not **first** paying attention to his blind master?

When walking at heel avoid looking at your dog, because when you turn your head to the left to look at him, you're actually walking crooked, thus causing him to pull away from you and also walk crooked. Walk straight keeping your eyes looking straight ahead, and view your dog only with your peripheral vision. The more relaxed you are, the more relaxed your dog will be. The leash tends to act as a conductor communicating to the dog your moment to moment demeanor. If you feel fearful, sad, happy, nervous or leery, your dog will very likely respond the very same way. So relax!

"**Z.**" Every time you stop, your dog should learn to **sit automatically.** (The **only exception** is if you were going to make him a **show dog,** in which case he should sit only on command.) He should sit and stay until another command is given. The reason for this is for **total control,** i.e. when you meet friends, you don't want the dog jumping on them, or going between their legs or around the telephone pole. You want the dog sitting or laying, but in either case, **staying.**

This lesson is a prelude to teaching Lesson 106, The Stay Command. During the second week of training, periodically have the dog sit or down and stay at the heel position for up to two minutes. Pretend you're talking to a friend. If the dog breaks at any time, put him right back down.

1. 90 degree sharp left turns. Make him yield to you!
Notice the "looseness" of the leash and its "proper" hold.

2. Keep moving. Bump-shock him if you have to.
Notice the "looseness" of the leash and its "proper" hold.

3. Left-about.
Notice the "looseness" of the leash and its "proper" hold.

4. Keep moving. Make him yield to you!
Notice the "looseness" of the leash and its "proper" hold.

5. Bump-shock him on his left if you have to.
Notice the "looseness" of the leash and its "proper" hold.

6. 90 degree left.
Notice the "looseness" of the leash and its "proper" hold.

7. Keep moving. Make him yield to you!
Notice the "looseness" of the leash and its "proper" hold.

The dog **must hold** his position until another command is given.

If only from the constant badgering of the family members, I've found that at the age of four to six months old, most dogs already know the Sit Command. If your dog doesn't know the "sit" command, he will by the end of this lesson.

Every time you stop, wait for five seconds, many dogs will naturally sit automatically, however, if yours doesn't, give the command **once**, "Prince...SSSSSIT!" If you already have his attention, do not use his name, simply give the command, "SSSSIT!" When giving the Sit Command, elongate the "S"..."SSSSIT!" You'll find that this is a more **shocking tone** and he'll respond better to it.

If, after five seconds, your dog does not sit, with your right hand, **casually**, grab a short leash (close to the collar); place your left hand on the **small of his back**; with your right hand, **firmly** and **shockingly** jerk (do not pull) **upwards and to the rear**, as your left hand shoves downward and to the rear, and you simultaneously command "SSSSIT!" **Hold** him in position for three seconds, then release the hold. If he breaks the position, repeat the procedure. If he holds the position, give praise in a soothing way. "Gooood boy! Gooood boy!" See page 197.

"SSSSIT!"

David and Champ
A. Turn slightly to the left.
B. Left hand on small of back.
C. Right hand on short leash.
D. Jerk upwards and to the rear, while
pushing downward and to the rear.

NOTE: When shoving the dog down and to the rear,
be sure that it is to the rear and not straight downward.
Because shoving straight downward could injure the dog.

When using this maneuver, **use judgment – don't be too heavy**, on the other hand, **don't be too lenient**. Being too lenient only causes the dog to resist, and afterwards, in the case of many dogs, a major battle would ensue every time you gave the Sit Command.

Follow these procedures and you'll find that in no time your dog will sit automatically within five seconds after stopping, and **certainly** within two weeks, **he will clearly know the "sit" command.**

WALKING TWO DOGS AT HEEL

For you folks that have two dogs and wish to walk them both at the same time, follow these tid-bits:

A. Do not attempt it until both dogs are fully trained.

B. Place both dogs at sit and stay on your left side – the heel position.

C. Use only one 6' leather leash.

D. Thread the handle of the leash through the loose ring (where the leash is normally attached) on the shock collar of one of the dogs.

E. Thread the catch of the leash along with the rest of the leash, through the handle. Pull the catch and the leash all the way through the handle until it tightens on the ring of the shock collar. Now you have one dog on leash the very same way as is normal except that the leash is reversed.

F. Attach the catch of the leash to the loose ring on the shock collar of your second dog. You now have both dogs on the same leash.

G. Place yourself at the heel position and grab only the doubled-up center of the leash. This gives both dogs the same amount (length) of leash.

H. Commence walking.

"Z." By using this method you will find that when jerks are necessary, the only dog that is affected is the one challenging—the one trying to get ahead of you—therefore, the method as a whole gives you much better control of your two dogs being walked at the same time...on the same leash. See page 200.

"HEEL!"

David, Champ and Sierra
Heel at the same time on the same leash.
Notice the "looseness" of the leash and its "proper" hold.

THE PERFECT HEEL

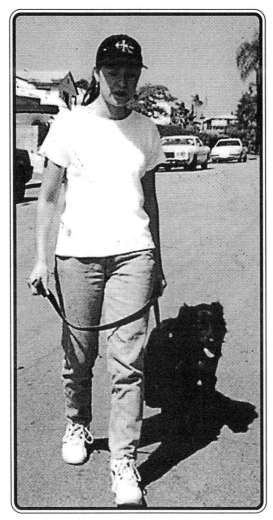

Edith and Morena
Notice the "looseness" of the leash and its "proper" hold.

DEFENDING AGAINST AN
ATTACKING STRAY DOG

Now that you are able to take your dog on controlled walks, you should also know that many dogs, especially small ones, have been maimed or killed by attacking, disgruntled stray dogs. Many of these attacks could have been stopped if people had known that these types of strays—one with an appetite for attack—usually do not rush to attack on sight of its prey – you and your dog. They usually stalk first, and then they attack. Therefore, in the majority of cases you know that it's going to happen, and this gives you a few seconds to prepare. Should you anticipate a problem, first try to calmly get away and avoid the situation. However, if you can't, do the following:

A. Immediately REVERSE the leash on your dog—as explained in "Walking Two Dogs With One Leash" (points A through D). With the leash's catch (the heavy metal portion) at the end of the leash, you now have a weapon.

B. Control you dog on a short leash with your left hand.

C. **Face** the oncoming stray and with your right hand, twirl the remaining leash as fast and furious as you can. Spin the leash in a wide circular manner, like an airplane propeller. This causes the leash to make a whizzing sound that is very **shocking** to the majority of dogs, and they will immediately back-off. If you encounter an attacking stray who does try to cross the line, have no mercy and let your weapon clank him! What do you think he will do now? ...You betcha' ...he will...run! See page 205.

D. For you small dog owners, simply pick-up and tightly hold your dog with your left hand and arm, snap off his leash, and with your right hand, swing the entire leach. In the majority of cases, even light weight leashes will work. Please see Mrs. Middleton's "success story" on page 4.

"**Z.**" Practice this maneuver before you get to the "combat zone." We have had students that called the very next day after we taught this maneuver, and some two years later, saying, "Guess what Dave, it worked wonders!" Practice, practice, practice – but be careful not to clank yourself or your dog.

TID-BITS TO PONDER AND REMEMBER

A. No more jerks, but shocking maneuvers.

B. Shock, does not mean hurt!

C. The Automatic Sit is to be developed. Use caution on

the dog's lower back when you place him.

    D. The basic maneuvers are:

       1. 90 degree left turns.

       2. 90 degree right turns.

       3. Circles to the left.

       4. Circles to the right.

       5. Figure eights.

       6. About-turns to the left.

       7. About-turns to the right.

       8. Zig-zag maneuvers.

    E. You may also combine **left obstacles crowding techniques** (which were taught in Lesson 104) when using any of the above maneuvers.

    F. To keep your dog **sharp and alert** on occasions vary the speed of your walks: run and come to abrupt stops, or drop to a lower gear, or to slow-motion, and then back to full speed, etc.

    G. Pick the right training area, especially at the beginning of training: the street, a parking lot, a tennis court - where there are less sniffs and distractions for the dog.

    "**Z.**" When your dog correctly responds for you, **do not forget the love factor, "GOOD BOY! GOOD BOY!"**

DR. JOSÉ MARIA GÓNZALEZ AHUAJE, D.D.S. AND ROBO-COP

Defending against an attacking stray dog!

THE SIT AND STAY COMMAND

"SSSSTAY!"

LESSON #106
THE SIT AND STAY COMMAND

In the previous lesson, your dog learned the Automatic Sit at Heel, and at the same time learned how to **hold the position** for at least two minutes. He now has basic knowledge of the Stay Command and teaching it **solidly** should now be easier for you. However, there are a few rules that **must** be followed.

A. In most cases, if you want to be sure **who** the leader is...it is determined by teaching **this** command! In other words, this is a maneuver which you can not show the dog your **insecurity**, because if you do, you can be certain that he'll sense it and make it very difficult for you.

Don't do as so many have done. How many times have you seen people, (or been guilty of it yourself,) when teaching the dog the Stay Command, waver and quiver, back and forth, to and from to the point of resembling a jumping bean, as they say to the dog, "Now puppy, you stay! Stay! Stay! Stay!" As they do this, they manage to move away from the dog a record setting six inches. The dog, seeing this totally neurotic individual, becomes puzzled and interprets the actions as such, and breaks his position. The master, as he jumps to grab the dog, wonders why. He tries again...and...back and forth...and back and forth they go. In many instances you could wonder, **who** is training **who** to do what?

When teaching the Stay Command, do not waver. Show the dog that you are sure of yourself and he will respond in kind. **The most important step in teaching this command is:** After you have given the Stay Command and you move away from the dog, should he break the stay position, **do not run back to him.** If you can't stop him with a firm "NO!" let him break. Let him come **all the way to you** or thereabouts, then **jerk** him, **swiftly,** all the way to where you first issued the command. If you allow **him** to draw **you** to him, you may never be able to teach him this command.

B. Do not use the dog's name, especially when you're first starting to teach the Stay Command. Why? To the dog, the use of the name signifies **action** and **movement** – "you want me to do something." In this case what do you want him to do? Basically, **nothing** but stay. In so many instances, I've seen people who manage to get about 4 or 5 feet away from the dog and say, "Now, Shadow, **you** stay!"

No sooner are the first two words said, and the dog comes running to them. **Do not** use the dog's name when giving the Stay Command.

C. Never bend at the waist or in any way lean over towards the dog. The dog interprets this as you **submitting** or **bowing** down to him and causes him to draw. Maintain your body **erect** at all times. **Cause the dog to look up at you, instead of you bowing down to him.**

D. Keep your hands **away** from the dog's nose, as this too will cause him to draw. Hands to a dog are like **magnets.**

"Z." After giving the Stay Command, move away from the dog leading with your **right foot**. Because, to the dog, leading with your **left foot** signifies the Heel Command.

TRAINING

A. Teaching the Stay Command begins with the dog at the sit-at-heel position.

B. Stand **erect** and with your **left** hand hold **only the handle** of the leash.

C. With the handle of the leash in your left hand, place

THE FIRST STEP

"SSSSTAY!"

your left hand on your waist. The rest of the leash should be dangling in the shape of a "U" between your left hand at the waist and the dog's neck.

D. Bring your **right** arm and hand across your chest, turn your body a **little** to the left, and holding your hand **palm down in front and above** the dog's head, **firmly** command him to "STAY!" For a more shocking tone, elongate the "S," "SSSSSTAY!" Remember, **do not** lean over. Hold this position for five seconds.

THE SECOND STEP

"SSSSTAY!"

E. Leading with your **right** foot and holding your **right** hand in front and above the dog's head, **pivot in front** of the dog. **You are now facing him.** In this position, give your command again, "SSSSTAY!" Hold this position for five seconds.

"SSSSTAY!"

"SSSSTAY!"

"SSSSTAY!"

"SSSSTAY!"

F. After five seconds, leading with your **right** foot, move **backwards** two feet. Give your hand signal and verbal command again. At this time, your arm and hand signal should resemble a **straight-arm**, forward, **short jab**. Hold this position for **fifteen** seconds.

G. After fifteen seconds, give your verbal and signal command again, and **immediately** return to the heel position. When returning to the heel position, **do not hesitate or waver**; at the same time, **reel** in your leash **keeping it loose** at all times.

H. After returning to the heel position, **hold** the position for five seconds, then praise your dog. **Don't be exuberant,** simply say, "Good boy. Good boy." with a **light** pat on the head.

The reason for **holding** the heel position for five seconds **before** praising your dog, is because if you were to praise him **immediately** on your return, he would, in subsequent tries, start **breaking** his position **in anticipation** of praise.

I. Take him for a **short walk** before returning to the **same** place you were and repeat the maneuver. Each time before doing this maneuver, you should take a **short** walk at heel.

J. Repeat the maneuver: Three times per session, **two days**; no more than three sessions per day.

K. For the **second two-day period**, repeat the maneuver as outlined; with the **exception** that now you should move **four feet** away from the dog and hold the position in front of him for **thirty seconds**.

L. For the **third two-day period,** move **six feet** away from the dog and hold the position for **forty-five seconds**. Make sure that you're keeping the leash very loose, because should the dog feel the **slightest tension,** his tendency would be to break towards you.

M. For the **fourth two-day period,** when you've reached your six foot distance, **maintain** the distance and walk a **semi-circle** in front of the dog. **Do not** go farther than the dog's left or right. Return to the heel position. This entire sequence should take no more or less than forty-five seconds.

N. For the **fifth two-day period,** the semi-circle you make should extend to the dog's left and right **peripheral** vision. Again this entire sequence should take no more or less than forty-five seconds.

O. By the **sixth two-day period,** you are now ready to do a **complete** circle around the dog, clockwise and counter-clockwise. He is used to you moving around him, but not directly in back of him, therefore:

1. Follow the steps as outlined to the point where you're standing six feet in front of the dog.

DREW CASTRO AND...
"SSSSTAY!"

The dog's vision requires movement.
Hand signals are not hand signals.

... MILLIE
"SSSSTAY!"

Hand signals are "body" language.
Exaggerate all signals. **Especially** when at a distance.
Notice the "looseness" of the leash and its "proper" hold.

2. Drop the leash.

3. Without hesitation, maintaining your six feet distance, make a complete circle around the dog. As you walk between the two peripheral points behind the dog, **speed up, almost run**, as you give the verbal command, "SSSSTAY!" Elapsed time – 45 seconds.

P. Following the steps as outlined, increase **the size** of the circle and **build** the Sit/Stay to two or three minutes— but **no more**. The reason for this is that the Sit/Stay position to a dog is a very **uncomfortable** position. They are almost **literally sitting** on their tailbone! Have you ever been to a theater and watched a 1 1/2 to 2 hour movie in a **slouched** position? At the end of the movie how did **your** tailbone feel? It's much worse for the dog; especially large dogs! With this in mind, as you are teaching the Sit/Stay Command, should your dog drop to the Down position, I suggest you **allow it**. The exception would be if you're going to make him a **show** dog, then it would **not** be permitted.

"Z." Since **you** are the one who is there working with your dog, **you** are the one who knows if he is easily understanding the Stay Command. If he is, and you want to speed-up the training between any of the given steps—**you** may make this decision.

At ABC School for Dogs, we usually have the students **start** teaching the Stay Command at steps L and M. Both are done on the same day, and **the majority** of the dogs respond very well. With the dogs that do not respond, we simply have the students start over from step A.

TID-BITS TO PONDER AND REMEMBER

A. Do not waver. Do not show **your** insecurities! Carry yourself, your commands, and the various steps you take, in an almost **slow motion** way. To the dog, this will make you appear **confident** and **sure** of yourself. The dog's tendency will be to respond **in kind!**

B. Do not use the dog's name.

C. Do not lean over. Stand erect at all times.

"Z." At any time, should the dog break position, **do not go running back to him.**

See page number 208 for **the most important step in teaching the Stay Command.**

"SSSSTAY!"

WINSTON, AT STEP "O".
Note that the **extended** leash
was dropped in front of the dog.

I cannot remember his exact words, but President Dwight D. Eisenhower once commented words to the effect that, " It is not the size of the dog in the fight — but the size of the fight in the dog."

You cannot become the Leader Of The Pack without the proper investment — read this book from cover to cover. The dividends derived by you will be unparalleled!

Happiness is... **A Better Canine!**

SU LING LIU'S YOGI

DEVIL OR ANGEL!

LESSON #107
SOLVING MISBEHAVIOR SITUATIONS

**CHEWING • BITING • BARKING • DIGGING • JUMPING ON
PEOPLE • JUMPING ON FURNITURE • DOOR CHARGING
• GETTING INTO TRASH • ETCETERAS!**

Through obedience training you have gained **your leadership** position over the dog and he should now be more **willing to listen** to you as it relates to misbehavior situations.

The main problem that we humans encounter in solving problems with our dogs is that the majority of the time, when we make a correction, the dog has **no idea** why they are being corrected. Picture the following two scenarios:

SCENARIO NO. 1 – CHARLES AND SALLY'S DOG

At 7:00 in the morning Charles goes to work, and at precisely 7:30 that morning, the dog goes to the bathroom in the middle of the living room – AGAIN! Sally spots the situation and hollers at the dog, "You bad dog, you wait until dad gets home tonight. You're going to get it!"

That evening Charles arrives home around nine, and no sooner does he walk through the door when Sally exclaims, "You know it wasn't half an hour after you left this morning, and that...that...that dog **of yours** went to the bathroom in the living room **again!**"

"Oh, he did, did he." Charles replied, as he walks into the living room. The dog is playing with a yellow rubber bone, tossing it in the air, and having a good ole' time. Charles kicks him and says, **"You bad dog, how many times do I have to tell you..."** And he kicks him again, and so on, and so on.

Well guess what? Six months later the dog is **still** going to the bathroom in the living room, **but he never again played with that yellow rubber bone.**

SCENARIO NO. 2 – MR. BANDITO'S DOG

We received a call from Mr. Bandito, who exclaimed, "Please help me, my dog is chewing **everything** in sight!" I went to his home to investigate and he welcomed me with, "Dave, I am telling you, it is **crazy** around here! He **chews** the coffee table, he **chews** the plants, he **chews** the hose...and...Dave, talk about the newspaper boy bringing the newspaper, if the dog gets a hold of it first, forget it, no paper! He **chews** it to bits!"

"Well, what do you do to correct him when he does all this damage?" I asked.

"Dave," he says, "I **beat** him! But he goes right back. He is just a **hardhead!**"

I asked Mr. Bandito to tell me **exactly** what he meant by **beating** him?

"I keep a rolled-up newspaper on top of the refrigerator, one by the trash can, and one by my chair. Every time he does it, I beat his butt royally! But he persists and goes right back to it!"

"Now wait a minute, Mr. Bandito, first you tell me that you beat him with a rolled-up newspaper! Could there **possibly** be a connection between that and why he chews your newspapers to bits? Also you say that you 'beat his butt!' – for chewing? Isn't **that** the wrong end?"

This is **precisely** what we humans do to our dogs. Perhaps not as exaggerated as these stories, but nevertheless, **just as bad!** There you have it...and on and on we go! The point is that you must learn to **match the discipline with the offense – there is no other way!** The dog must know why he is being corrected. There **must** be a connection made between the **discipline** and the **offense.**

There are two basic misbehavior situations:

1. When you **catch** the dog in the act.

2. **After-the-fact** situations – when you come home and find the damage.

It is true, **very true,** that a dog learns better when you catch him in the act. But it is **also true** that you **can** correct after-the-fact, even if it's twelve hours later. **You can and you should!** In other words, **never let anything go un-checked,** because as sure as you do, it's **negative training.** The more he does it, the more he does it! It goes **unchecked**...the more he does it.

In many cases it becomes a matter of who is smarter. So this is what you do. Set-up the dog in the misdeed situation, catch him in the act, and make your correction. Now you stand a better chance of solving the situation. With this in mind, let's first talk about situations when you catch the culprit in the act.

TRAINING

CORRECTING MISBEHAVIORS WHEN YOU CATCH THE DOG IN THE ACT

THE BOOMERANG TECHNIQUE

A. When you catch the culprit in the act, nothing but nothing works better than what I've named "The Boomerang Technique." In some dog training circles, similar methods are used with various other names. See example of boomerangs in Lesson 103, page 150.

The Boomerang Technique is simply the use of three small (six ounce) tin (works better than aluminum) cans, filled with about twelve pennies or a few stones (pennies are best.) The boomerangs do not necessarily have to be tin cans. Some students have used small homemade bean bags, or to keep the tin cans from marring furniture or floors as they are thrown, concealed them in foam rubber thermos containers. These tools are amazingly successful in solving your dog's misbehaviors. **BUT ONLY, I repeat, ONLY if you use them properly.**

B. So...what is properly? Let's say the dog is chewing the hose, or he's about to jump on someone, he's digging a hole in the yard, or he's on your favorite chair. Using the last example, he's on your favorite chair, and you've told him 1001 times to, "GET OFF THE CHAIR!" but he persists. Now, however, you know about the trusty Boomerang Technique. So you grab the boomerangs, all three of them, you've caught him in the act, and you swiftly (remember to use judgment in the degree of force) throw the boomerangs at him, one right after the other as you command, "GET OFF THAT CHAIR!" **The moment** he comes off the chair, you must move in on the chair (or whatever object it is, plant, hole, etc.) and strike or shake that item over and over. Hit the chair, shake the plant or pick-up some of the dirt where he was digging, as you emphatically command, "THIS IS A NO! NO! NO! NO! NO!" Follow this with **negative reinforcement** (see next section), as you point to the situation, you command, "DO **YOU** WANT TO GET UP HERE AGAIN? DO **YOU** WANT TO DIG THIS HOLE AGAIN? DO **YOU** WANT TO CHEW THIS AGAIN? DO **YOU** WANT TO JUMP ON HER AGAIN?"

C. **When using the boomerangs, use them exactly as described and only for the first five misdeed situations.** I repeat – only for the first five misdeed situations. Not five times for each situation, but five times only. Two or three of the five situations can be the same situation. It may take you five hours or five months to arrive at the fifth time. **Only five times means only five times! Period!**

After using the boomerangs as instructed for five times, for the remainder of the life of the dog, you are to use them on a **positive threat basis** only! **Positive threat basis** means that on the 6th or 6006th misdeed, you only threaten to throw the boomerangs, and throw only if you have to. With boomerangs in hand, you threaten to throw in the direction of the misbehavior. If the dog doesn't instantaneously correct himself, you throw. **Again, if the dog doesn't instantaneously correct himself, you throw and follow through.** The throw is the positive of the positive threat basis formula. However, in the majority of cases, you'll find that the necessity of a sixth throw is remote. If your dog doesn't respond instantaneously to the threat, you can be sure that it is for two reasons:

1. He has no respect for the boomerangs. Chances are that you have not used them properly.

2. He has much less respect for you. He is a hard-core juvenile delinquent!

As I've explained, **dogs —all dogs—are very susceptible to shock.** At Qualcomm Stadium in San Diego, fireworks are sometimes set off after a ball game, and I've known dogs that live in that area, to go into a frenzy and run away. Others simply become paranoid and try to climb walls, and if they can get into the house, end up crouched and trembling in a secluded area such as the bathtub or the farthest corner of a closet. This also happens throughout the country where thunderstorms are prevalent.

IN THE CARE AND TRAINING OF YOUR DOG, ALWAYS REMEMBER THE DOG'S SUSCEPTIBILITY TO SHOCK.

"Z." We have many students who tell us that when their dog begins to misbehave, all they do is point at the boomerangs, and instantly the dog settles down. The boomerangs are very effective, **but ONLY if you use them properly.**

NEGATIVE REINFORCEMENT FORMULA

A. Essentially what you are doing when you use negative reinforcement is daring the dog to do it again – whatever the misbehavior was. You'll find the negative reinforcement technique most effective, especially if you simultaneously express your daring remarks and grab the dog by the collar, and in a **quick, dazzling** and **shocking way, pull him toward** the misdeed. You'll find that his tendency will be to **pull away from** the situation. When pulling him toward the situation, be sure not to outdo him. Let him struggle (pull away) for about five seconds, then let him go, followed immediately with a firm tone, "NOW YOU BE A GOOD BOY!" Then simultaneously a small pat on the head and a passive friendly tone, "Now you be a good boy!"

B. Important to know: In situations when you catch the dog in the act or misdeed and use of negative reinforcement, you **do not have to grab** and pull him toward the situation every time. In most cases, just your negative or daring remarks will do. However, if it's a **recurring situation** that needs to be reinforced, **do grab** him and pull him toward the situation.

C. Negative reinforcement tones also work before the fact. Many of our students have corroborated this, as Joe and Gail did with this story:

"We bought a new planter for the coffee table. (Max, their 105 lb. Japanese Akita, had destroyed the old one). I grabbed Max by his collar and took him to the new planter on the table. I pulled him towards the planter as I sternly commanded, 'DO YOU WANT TO CHEW THIS? DO YOU? THIS IS A NO! NO! NO!' Max has never again gone even near the planter."

"Z." Using negative reinforcement tones during the act.

The following story illustrates how negative reinforcement and the Boomerang Technique was used effectively in the case of Alex and Beverly, and their Doberman Pin-scher, Peppie:

"We're about to be evicted if we don't stop her from barking all day long. The neighbors keep complaining. We've hollered at her many times and we've tried the electric shock collar. Nothing seems to work."

I visited with these folks and found that the problem stemmed from the fact that Alex and Beverly had no control over the dog whatsoever! I explained to them that a dog **as a rule does not bark all day long,** and when they do bark, there is usually a reason, or a draw.

Our meeting took place on a Friday, so fortunately we had the weekend to immensely improve the situation and halt any eviction notices. That evening we had our first session, "The Psychology of How the Dog Learns." Alex and Beverly could not believe how wrong they had been; how quickly a dog learns; and how bad or should we say, how well Peppie had **them** trained!

Before the night was over, Peppie no longer jumped on the furniture; did not charge the front door; was not in the way of where anyone walked; and could almost walk decently on a leash without pulling. **Leadership reversal had definitely taken place!**

Regarding Peppie's excessive barking, we found that it only took place whenever someone walked by the alley, which was about seventy-five feet from the back porch of the house, and where the dog stayed during the day. When someone walked by, Peppie would charge. She looked like a torpedo, and she always zeroed-in on an already weakened area of the fence. She barked, growled and snarled.

On Saturday morning, we set her up. I had Alex and Beverly get into their car and pretend to leave. I met them down the street and we walked to the house. Alex and I snuck into the house and waited. It wasn't long before someone walked by the alley, and Peppie, like a bat out of hell, charged. No sooner did she get to the fence, when Alex and I like gangbusters, jumped out of the back door, firing boomerangs at her. I ran to the fence and as she tried to run away, I grabbed her and proceeded to shove and pull her toward the fence. I shook and shook the fence. During the entire process, I commanded in a very stern manner, "DO YOU WANT TO GET UP HERE AGAIN? DO YOU WANT TO BARK OVER HERE? THIS IS A NO! NO! NO! NO!"

During the week, Alex and Beverly performed the set-up again, implanting into Peppie's mind that the barking would only bring a very shocking and uncomfortable consequence. *As a result, three weeks later, Alex and Beverly were*

evicted for creating too much racket with the throwing of the boomerangs – and if you believe this, I have some prime property near Ft. Myers, Florida that I want to sell to you.

SOLVING RECURRING MISBEHAVIORS WHILE AWAY FROM HOME
Barking, Howling, Destructiveness, etc.

A. As with Peppie, if your dog is notorious while you're away from home, pay him a few surprise "social" calls. Remember, when you appear, it must be like **gangbusters!** Setting him up a few times is the only way to resolve these types of misbehaviors. We have implanted into the dog's mind that **his undesired actions are what caused you to appear!**

B. Some students have expressed hesitation with the use of boomerangs. "You mean to tell me Dave, that you want me to throw these things right at my puppy?"

"Absolutely!" I tell them. Why right at him? First, if you hit him, you're not going to hurt him; not with a "little ole' tin can" that doesn't weigh anything. That's if you hit him. Secondly, in 95% of the cases, unless you happen to be a very good throw, you're going to miss him – you are in the heat of battle and you have a moving target. Even if you land close, it's still effective. In any event, remember, that you're **never out to hurt the dog;** you're **only** out to **shock** him.

"Z." Why the Boomerang Technique? You know what a real boomerang is – you throw it and it comes back to you. For our training purposes, you throw the boomerangs and the **dog comes back** to the correct behavior; he **comes away** from the misbehavior. Hence, the Boomerang Technique.

CAUTION USING THE BOOMERANG TECHNIQUE

How powerful is the Boomerang Technique? In solving problems with your dog, this technique is so powerful that it is imperative that caution be used with its use, or I should say over use. Let me state this again: **The Boomerang Technique is so powerful** that **caution** and **good judgment** must be employed with its use. **DO NOT OVER USE THIS TECHNIQUE WITH YOUR DOG!** Why? Because this technique is so **shock** effective, that if you were to over use it, you could make your dog neurotic. You could literally drive him crazy! We have seen it before, fortunately **never** with one of our students. **We go to extreme lengths to make certain that they/you know the proper way of using this technique.** One of my pet peeves in this business has been finding the Boomerang Technique (also referred to by various other names) written about in books, but **never** with a **full** explanation, and certainly **never** expressing the **dangers** of its use.

Previously we talked about Sasha, a German Shepherd imported from Germany to National City, California. Boomerang-type techniques were over used on her from the time that she was just a puppy. When I was called onto the case, at the dog's golden age of a mere seven months, she

"NO! NO! NO!"
Point C., Page 239

was already an irreversible neurotic. The sight of a neurotic dog is not a pleasant thing to see; the eyes are fixed, the dog is not responsive to any commands, he/she paces back and forth, and every unusual sound puts them into a frenzy. Sasha had to be put to sleep.

TRAINING

CORRECTING MISBEHAVIORS AFTER THE FACT

What do most people do when correcting, or should I say, attempting to correct an after-the-fact situation? What do most people do when they come home and find:

A. The dog ate the stamp collection or the Bible that has been in the family for 150 years.

B. The piano is no longer sitting on four legs, but laying on its side on two.

C. Their home looks like a tornado went through it.

What do most people do? Let me share with you what James and Sylvia's dog, Greta, experienced. One early afternoon, James and Sylvia arrived home only to find that Greta had eaten their brand new couch. I saw the couch, and Greta had totally and completely demolished it. She had even scooted it away from the wall and ate the back of it – only the frame was left! On seeing this, James, a burly bubba-type fellow, took off his belt and proceeded to severely beat the dog for quite some time. Then he threw Greta in a closet for about two hours; brought her out and severely beat her again. He threw her outside, where she remained for the rest of the night. Sylvia threatened divorce if he ever again did this to the dog. At this point, I was brought in.

This is a true story, depicting not what most people do, but similar. People rant, rave and throw the dog out. So what should you do? What is the correct way of correcting after-the-fact?

CORRECTING CORRECTLY AFTER-THE-FACT
PART I

A. Before starting after-the-fact corrections, you must first **clear the dog's brain**. As in working a calculator, you'll never get the correct results unless you first clear the mechanism.

When you first walk in the door, regardless of the damage you're looking at, you must ignore it. Welcome the puppy in a normal manner, "Hi puppy, yes I love you puppy." You don't need to overdo the greeting, be as **natu-**

ral as possible. If you begin hollering at the dog when you first walk in, he'll have no knowledge of why you're upset. Also, never holler at your dog in any area other than the exact area where the "crime" was committed. Remember, the "coming home hour" should always be a "happy hour."

B. Proceed by putting him on leash. In the area of the scene of the crime, put him through his paces: "Heel, sit; good boy. Stay; good boy. Heel, sit..." This should take but a few seconds.

C. Continue by heading toward "the scene of the crime" and stop with the dog in front of it, and as you point to it, in a low tone, you exclaim, "WHAT IS THIS? DID YOU DO THIS?" What you're doing is pretending as if you just found the damage. In the majority of cases, at this juncture the dog will cower. Continue by grabbing his muzzle (mouth) with your right hand (if your dog is too powerful for you or has an aggressive nature, use **caution** and wrap your leash around his mouth—like a muzzle— grab and tighten the leash under his mouth). With your left hand grab his head—the scruff area. Be sure that you have a good grip on him. Put his nose into the situation. (The **exception** to this is never put his nose into his own feces. This would be totally unfair and unsanitary. You can put his nose one thousandth of an inch near his feces, but **never touching it**.) Rub his nose into the situation, then ram his nose into it about eight or ten times, as you forcefully command, "THIS IS A NO! NO! NO! NO! NO!" The force of the ramming comes from the movement of your hands and arms, not the actual contact of the dog's nose into the hard object. We are not telling you to "go for blood." You must always use **good judgment**, especially if it's a hard object. On the other hand, remember the formula of a loving, fair and good correction – firm, sharp and to the point. Get it over with! During the entire correction, the dog is struggling to get away.

D. You want to make a scene at the "scene of the crime." Show your wrath, make a display. This will help the correction, because your dog would rather perceive you as the provider of hugs, kisses and cookies. So, make a scene at the scene!

"Z." Keeping hold of the end of the leash, release your hold on him. He'll go to the end of the leash, as you use negative reinforcement tones (you are now pointing to and slightly pulling him towards the scene of the crime), "DO YOU WANT TO DO THIS AGAIN, DO YOU? DO YOU?" Then come back to passive love, "Now you be a good boy. Be a good boy." This is the end of the first part of the correction; now turn him loose. The second part is the **soaking-in time period.**

CORRECTING CORRECTLY AFTER-THE-FACT
PART II
THE SOAKING-IN TIME PERIOD

A. This means that for at least the next 45 minutes, you should not do anything with the dog. In other words, to the extent that a dog can remember or relate, allow him to remember and relate during this time. Let him soak it in. As one student put it, "Let it marinate." During this soaking-in period, do not feed him, do not give him a cookie, do not take him for a walk. If you made the correction indoors, do not throw him out – leave him indoors. If you made the correction outdoors, do not allow him to come indoors – leave him outdoors. During the soaking-in period, always keep him in the area of "the scene of the crime."

B. For hard-core or recurring situations, don't hesitate to tie the dog down (one foot of leash only) to the scene of the crime, i.e. the piano leg he chewed, the hole he dug, the trash can he got into, the cupboard door where you keep the trash, etc.

"Z." Some students have asked, "Dave, let's say that we didn't find the damage until seven hours after the dog did it. Does he really know why he was corrected?"

My response is, "Of the five senses, which one is the

**SU LING LIU
AND YOGI**

這些是什麼?

("What...is all this!")

Su Ling Liu corrects
Yogi after he destroyed
all her plants in the
patio.

不行! 不行! 不行!

("NO! NO! NO!")

Let him struggle...
but, don't let him win!

不行! 不行! 不行!

("NO! NO! NO!")

Time elapsed in the correction: no more than 12 to 15 seconds!

不行! 不行! 不行!

("NO! NO! NO!")

most powerful sense of the dog?" Who went to the bathroom in the middle of the living room? Who spent time gnawing on that piece of furniture? What's the dog going to do? Blame it on the kitty-cat or one of the kids? What is the most **powerful** sense of the dog? How are you making the correction? Believe me when I tell you that I'm convinced that in 95% of the cases, the dog knows **'through the nose'** – he knows! In the other 5% of the cases, your correction is creating an aversion, so it's still a good correction."

As I have asked my students, I ask you, "If we were to believe that you can only correct a dog when you catch him 'in the act,' would we ever solve any problems with our dog?" When does a dog usually misbehave anyhow? Make your correction. We don't care if it's 12 hours after the fact. **Make your correction!** In other words, **never** let anything go **unchecked**, otherwise it's negative training. The more he "does it" and you don't say anything, the more he "does it." However, on the other hand, as much as you possibly can, do not give your dog the opportunity to misbehave. Remember **supervision, confinement and control.**

Su Ling Liu and her children, Shawn and Michelle, of Rancho Penasquitos, California regarding their heinz-variety, Yogi, "With this type of training, won't he start hating us and try to get even, or burn the house down?"

A DOG'S MEMORY
DO DOGS HAVE A SHORT MEMORY?

Let me tell you about Honey, my female German Shepherd/Keeshond and a situation that she remembered though several years had passed. I "inherited" Honey at about the age of nine months. She was wild, a runaway-type dog, an escape artist, who also loved to chase kitty-cats. Her owners and I chased her for miles and hours around the area she lived in, Bonita, California, a suburb of San Diego. She was cuter than a punkin', and I fell in love with her the first time I saw her. In spite of her cuteness, her owners, a Mexican family, quickly gave up on her. Honey was just too much to handle. I always seem to end up with the hardheads!

At the time I was living in a second story apartment. Downstairs there was a court yard and a redwood gate that led to the parking lot and an open field. This is where the dogs went to the bathroom. Shortly after Honey arrived, as I slept, one very early morning 2:30 a.m. or so, Honey jumped on my bed and shoved me with her front paws. I awoke and thought that she must have to go to the bathroom. As I'm normally a very sound sleeper and do not like to be disturbed (in fact on occasions I've been accused of being grumpy when I wake-up, but between you and me, don't believe it), reluctantly, I stumbled out of bed and took Honey downstairs. As I opened the gate to let her into the field, she charged, giving chase to a kitty-cat! Up the alley they went and Honey was gone! I went back upstairs, put on my trousers, came back downstairs, got into my car and away I went looking for her. An hour and a half later, I'm back with Honey...in tow!

Several nights later it happened again. Honey jumped on the bed and nudged me. I awoke, turned to her, grabbed her by the scruff and firmly shoved her off, shook her and commanded, "YOU GO TO SLEEP! Now you BE a good girl! Go to sleep!" I rolled over and quickly went right back to sleep. A moment later, Honey came back and nudged me again. I thought perhaps this time she really does have to go to the bathroom. I'll give her the benefit of the doubt. I got up, went downstairs and opened the gate. Guess what! Away went Honey, chasing that same kitty-cat! Once again, an hour or so later I'm back with Honey...in tow!

About one week passed, and it happened **one more time.** This time as Honey nudged me, I rolled over, pretended to be asleep, and positioned myself in a way that I could make a **firm** correction. She nudged me again, as she did, I quickly turned and as severely as I could, put my elbow into her chest. She crashed and "bounced off the wall." I got to my feet, grabbed her by the scruff, and in a dazzling way, shook her, as I firmly placed her on the floor and commanded, "NOW YOU GO TO SLEEP! GO TO SLEEP! You be a good girl."

Honey **never** jumped on my bed again. But, several years later, in the fall when the time changed, Honey, of course, didn't know that it had changed. I usually feed her and the other guys about 6:00 a.m. so for all they knew I had overslept. Somehow they had to communicate to me, "Hey dad, get up, it's chow time! We're hungry!" As I slept, Honey came to my face...AND...EVER...SO...GENTLY, with the very tip of her tongue, licked my eye lids. First one, then the other. "Lick, lick! Lick, lick!" The gentleness of her licks were almost as if a butterfly had landed on my eyelids. I slightly opened my eyes, realizing the sweetness of what was going on, I ignored her. (Rambo, my male German Shepherd, was standing by, ears half way down with a worried look on his face, as if waiting for the **explosion** to go off.) Again Honey licked my eyelids, first one, then the other. "Lick, lick! Lick, lick!" I GOT UP...HUGGED THEM...AND FED THEM. Although this happened years later, did Honey remember the consequences of shoving? You betcha' she did! **Do dogs have a short memory? I don't think so!**

USING BALLOONS
TO SOLVE PROBLEMS

During this lesson, some students will have problems such as, "Dave, my dog doesn't just dig, he excavates, and it's always as if he was digging to China and always in the same place. I fill it in and the next day he digs it out. This has been going on for months. So how am I going to solve it?"

"Get some heavy-duty balloons. Put a little talcum powder or flour into one of them, blow it up tight and bury it where the dog digs. If you have to, make the hole larger to accommodate the balloon. Bury it and level it off with loose dirt about two inches above the balloon. What do you think will happen?"

The discussion continues, with the student asking, "After the dog experiences the first balloon, what's to tell him not to go elsewhere to dig?"

"What was the dog doing when he experienced the 'earthquake?' What's to tell him that elsewhere he isn't going to 'strike oil?' Visualize it."

Robert's red Doberman Pincher, Roxanne, when she is outside loves to jump up on the windows. When I arrived at Robert's home, he grabbed my arm as he lead me to the windows of his home to show me what Roxanne had done. "Dave, look at my windows. Look at the mud on them. Every one of them! By the time I get out there to catch her in the act, she runs away!"

For our next lesson, I had him get some balloons. When I arrived, we immediately went to the back steps. I took the first balloon and blew it up tight. You know how curious dogs can get about almost everything. No sooner had Roxanne put her nose on the balloon, when I popped it. As I did this, I simultaneously jumped back in horror as it exploded. Roxanne was nowhere to be seen. She ran as fast and as hard as she could to the side of the house. I took a second balloon, blew it up tight and proceeded to use it to play catch with Robert.

From the side of the house, Roxanne was keeping a very cautious and watchful eye, and every time the balloon went her way, she disappeared into the farthest corner. Periodically, she would draw out to check the situation, then run back. I waited until she drew towards us as much as she was going to, which wasn't very far, and I popped a second balloon. I had Robert tape a balloon on each one of his windows. Do you think Roxanne jumps up on the windows anymore?

Using this technique can appear that you're having one very long party as you may need to continue with the balloons for one month. At least the pattern is broken, and with follow-up training the problem is always solved. Balloons work very well in many situation, if only we use **a little imagination.**

USING MOUSE TRAPS TO SOLVE PROBLEMS

Tony and Beatrice have a Golden Retriever named Brandon. "Dave, he never gets on our bed when we're home. But when we're gone...the hair, the dirt...we know he's been up there. How are we going to solve this problem if we're not there to catch him?

"Mouse traps!" I tell them. "You go purchase about ten mouse traps, not rat traps, but mouse traps—small ones for small dogs, medium ones for large dogs. Just before you leave, set them and strategically place them on your bed."

Some students are concerned with the use of mouse traps. "Won't they hurt the dog, and is it really fair to have the traps **on him** until we get home?"

In the years that I've been training dogs, I can attest to the fact that **NEVER** have I known of a dog that was hurt by the use of mouse traps. **NEVER** have I heard of a student that arrived home and found a mouse trap **on** their dog. I assure you that when using mouse traps, it is extremely doubtful that the trap would ever snap closed on the dog. In the unlikely event that it did, it would not hurt the dog; plus he would readily and immediately remove it.

Some dog trainers will advise you to put newspapers on top of the mouse traps. The crinkling of the newspaper supposedly creates more of a shock, and protects the dog from getting hurt. Personally, I don't believe it, however, **you do** as your conscience dictates.

Mouse traps have been used for hundreds of years to solve problems with dogs. The **shock value** for many situations i.e. the dog gets into the kitchen or bathroom trash, gets up on or reaches the kitchen counter or even the window sill, keeps digging in your favorite planter, etc. is unparalleled. Mouse traps can also be used for digging.

When solving misbehavior situations with your dog, always keep in mind, **"How can I shock him?"** Always remember to **shock** the dog **in** the undesired situation. The dog avoids the situation because of the **shock** that went with it. As one student put it, "In other words Dave, **we** go around **biting** the dog!"

Also remember this fact: Not all dogs are created equal! Some are more hardheaded, some more dominant, and some are just plain hard-core juvenile delinquents. Not all problems will be solved with just one correction; some will take two, and some one hundred and two. **You must stay with it. Don't let him wear you out. Don't let him win!**

Naomi is one of the finest human beings I know. She's easy going in all respects, a true, beautiful lady. She called for training her 8-month-old, highly exuberant, dominant, full-blooded, 80 pound male German Shepherd, named Hero. To try to get near Hero was to take your life in your own hands, let alone try to walk him! But Naomi wanted him trained, especially to be a gentle companion to her five-year-old son, Chris.

For better than a year, I spent most of my Wednesday mornings with Naomi, Chris and Hero. Hero was a definite challenge, a true juvenile delinquent. In many situations such as kitty-cat chasing, running away, aggressively jumping on people, and acting like a wild hooligan while in the car, Hero required much work and many, many corrections. Naomi didn't give up on him.

We worked **very** hard with Hero, and as time passed, the proof was in the pudding. Not only could Naomi walk

Hero at a perfect heel and have full control of him, but to a great extent, so could Chris, who with Hero, became not only great companions, but also **the best of friends!**

If one type of correction doesn't work with your particular dog, try another method. **Not all methods work the same way with all dogs.** I've seen dogs that purposely burst balloons, and love it! Some dogs will deliberately set off mouse traps, and eat them! **If one method doesn't work, try another. There is no such thing as not winning over your dog!**

DEBORAH WHITNEY AND JORDAN

"NO! NO NO!"

Negative Reinforcement:

"DO YOU WANT TO DO THIS AGAIN!"

FORMULA FOR EXTRA
CHALLENGING SITUATIONS

After what seemed like months and many severe corrections on her dog, Islay, for digging, Susan said to me, "Dave, have you ever known of a dog that **could not** be broken of digging?"

"Susan, there is no such thing." and I proceeded with these instructions. "Fill in this last hole and starting tomorrow, if Islay digs, you're to make the most severe correction you can muster. Make him eat the dirt, make him hate it! Do not fill in the hole. Then make the same correction for the same hole three hours later, and again three hours after that."

The exact formula is: Three corrections a day for three days, every three hours. After the third day, fill in the hole and subsequently, if he digs, apply the formula **again**; and if necessary, **again**. This same formula can be applied to any extra challenging situation.

If we were to meet Susan today, she would brag to you about her **beautiful garden**, and her **wonderful dog**. For a lay person, Susan, in spite of physically being a very small woman, is one of the finest dog handlers I've seen. By the way, Islay is a male Golden Retriever, who during training was six-months-old and weighed sixty-five pounds.

WHO IS SMARTER?

In many cases when solving problems with your dog, it may seem to arrive at the point of, "Who is smarter?!" Use your imagination. There is always a way in which you can **shock and knock out your challenger**.

A. Take for example, Mrs. Alexis and Schipperkee, Molly. Mrs. Alexis liked having various handmade, crochet, personalized towels hanging from several places in her kitchen and bathroom. For Molly this was just one more temptation. She would jump and pull them down – all of them. Molly also did the same with toilet paper! Every chance she got, she would string it out all over the house.

I had Mrs. Alexis balance **boomerangs** on top of the towels and toilet paper. Molly didn't have to reach for the towels and toilet paper very many times before she got the idea when boomerangs "bounced" all around her.

B. Ervin and Pauline's black Labrador Retriever, Sam, kept getting and chewing the books on the shelf. They balanced **boomerangs** on a couple of the shelves, and for Sam, that was enough of a deterrent.

C. Donald and Christina live in Lakeside, California and are the owners of Boston Terriers, Pheobe and Benny. Christina called me, "Dave, what am I going to do? Phoebe and Benny keep going to the bathroom in their crate during the night. One, two, three o'clock in the morning, they begin crying, squealing and carrying on because of the mess they've made, and I have to get up to clean it up! What can I do?"

I instructed her as follows, "Tonight, just before you go to bed, take Phoebe and Benny to their bathroom area, and before putting them in their crate, take the pillows and blankets out and have them sleep without them. If they go to the bathroom and begin crying and carrying on at whatever ungodly hour, let them! You ignore them. Roll over and go to sleep. Do this every night until they realize the consequences of their misdeed."

Several weeks later, I received the following report from Christina, "It was hard to follow through, Dave. They cried and whimpered and shook the crate. **They almost got to me.** But as best I could, I rolled over and went to sleep. One night was all it took. Phoebe and Benny have never gone to the bathroom in their crate again!"

"**Z.**" As I arrived at Bob's house in Rancho Penasquitos, California, he welcomed me with, "Dave, my wife is ready to kill you, me and the dog, if we don't keep him out of her flower bed!"

It happened that their entire yard was pool area except a corner where they had built a flower bed about 3' off the ground. Well, where did Macho, an 8-month-old, male, Golden Retriever, choose to lie, sleep, and dig? I asked Bob if he had a mouse trap. He did. I put Macho on the leash, took him to the flower bed and set the mouse trap. I showed it to him as I commanded, "DO YOU SEE THIS! DO YOU! DO YOU!" and I made it go off on his nose. With Macho now bucking like a bronco, as best I could, I again set the trap and made it go off. For a third time I set the mouse trap and commanded, "DO YOU SEE THIS!" As I placed the trap in the flower bed, I picked him up and tried to shove him into the mouse trap sitting in the flower bed. I continued to command, "DO YOU WANT TO GET IN HERE AGAIN! DO YOU! DO YOU!" Macho is now furiously peddling backwards! I turned him loose and he ran to the other end of the yard, and as he did, I made a big issue of the flower bed. "This is a NO! NO! NO! NO! Now you BE a good puppy! BE a good puppy!"

We did that trick with Macho probably eight years ago. Bob told me that he took the mouse trap out of there that same afternoon, but I assure you that as far as Macho is concerned, that mouse trap is still there!

USE YOUR IMAGINATION – THERE IS ALWAYS A WAY YOU CAN SHOCK AND KNOCK-OUT YOUR CHALLENGER!

USING SHORT-CUTS
TO SOLVE PROBLEMS

Some dogs are **notorious** about a particular situation. You may want to "short-cut" it.

A. Digging: Lay chicken wire in the area. It works wonders!

B. Jumping the fence: Your local pet store can supply you with what is called a **Fido-Shock**. This is a wire that carries a **light** electrical current. Install it around the perimeter where you don't want the dog to cross. The dog touches it—and will **never** touch it again! I've seen this method work miracles in many situations!

C. Mouse traps and balloons are short-cuts.

"Z." In Lesson 102, we talked about "the biting" effect. Remember? In the case of the dog that leaped into the refrigerator – who "bit" the dog? In the case of the dog that was chewing the table – who "bit" the dog? Therefore:

1. If the dog jumps on you, what should "bite" him? The knee – very shockingly!

2. If the dog chews on the shoe strings of a shoe you're wearing, what should "bite" him? The shoe!

3. If the dog chews on a shoe which he got out of the closet, what should "bite" him? The shoe! How? You **casually** walk past him, and as you do, **you** kick the shoe. This drives the shoe into his mouth. So what "bit" the dog? The shoe!

4. If the dog is always "under foot"—walk through him! Accidentally, on purpose **step on him!** Who "bit" the dog?

Get the idea? But don't forget the love. **SHOCKLOVE!**

THIS LAST POINT SHOULD BE NOTED ESPE-CIALLY BY "YOU" THE ELDERLY. SAVE YOUR-SELF THE TRAUMA OF A BROKEN HIP AND/OR OTHER BONES AND LONG HOSPITAL STAYS, AS SO MANY OTHERS HAVE EXPERIENCED — IF ONLY THEY HAD KNOWN … "THE TRUTH!"

DEFINITION AND EXAMPLES OF
AVERSION EXPERIENCES

Notice that throughout the examples that have been given to solve problems an **aversion** was created for the dog. Just **exactly** what is an aversion, especially as it relates to solving our dogs' **notorious** misbehaviors? An aversion is the creation of a **counteracting happening** which the dog **never** wants to experience again. As one student simply put it, "In other words Dave, the essence of what you're talking about is a little bit of 'Tough Love' huh?" That's right, **Tough Love**! Take for example these scenarios:

A. Christy and Carl are a senior citizen couple who gave up training their little white toy poodle, J.C. "He's driving us crazy, Dave. Would you please train him for us. We just can't handle him!"

On one occasion, at my home, I wanted J.C., Rambo, and Honey outside to do their business. I commanded, "Rambo, out!" Rambo went out. "Honey, out!" Honey went out. "J.C., out!" In a challenging, "catch-me-if-you-can" manner, J.C. looked up at me, looked up the hallway, back at me, and like a locomotive, away he went, up the hallway, into the bedrooms, and back out to the living room, where again he gave me that same look. In a stern manner, I commanded, "J.C., OUT!" But J.C. ... away he went, "catch-me-if-you-can!" I sat down on the couch which is near the doorway. Thinking that he had won the battle, it didn't take long before J.C. was up there with me. I grabbed him by his little scruff, stood up, firmly shook him, at the same time commanding, "OUT!" I flung him out the door. He looked like a small bowling ball rolling out. "Now you BE a good boy!"

The next day, the same situation. I commanded, "Rambo, out!" Rambo went out. "Honey, out!" Honey went out. "J.C. ..." and before I could even give the command, all that one could see was a streak of white going out the door. A little bit of "tough love" goes a long way. After that, White Lightening should have been J.C.'s name.

B. One time while attending a convention in Atlanta, Georgia, I had Prince with me. I took Prince out to a field near the hotel where I was staying. While going about his business, Prince apparently went too close to a tree where a Blue Jay had his nest. The Blue Jay came swooping down and struck Prince on the head. Talk about a shocking aversion—one of the darndest things I ever saw! As to Prince...**never** to go near that tree again.

"Z." A student told the following story about what her father did to her dog and her brother when they were kids on the farm:

"Our dog kept getting into the trash drums—the 50 gallon type. One day Dad got fed up with it, took the dog, stuffed him in a drum and rolled him down a hill. The dog **never** got near the trash drums again!"

In just about the same breath, she went on about the story of her brother and his prolonged "sittings" in the bathroom.

"It seemed that every time one of the family members wanted to go to the bathroom, my brother was in there. He used to spend hours in there. It was a major battle every time. Until one day Dad walked to the bathroom and created an aversion for my brother. He put his foot through the door, opened it, grabbed my brother by the "scruff" of his neck and put his head in the toilet, flushed it and held him there. Dad, in no uncertain terms commanded, 'TWO MINUTES!' My brother **never** again repeated his notorious habit."

I share these stories with you exactly the way they were told to me. Although I don't totally agree with their exaggerated manner, they **do** exemplify the meaning of an **aversion**.

TID-BITS TO PONDER AND REMEMBER

A. You must match the discipline with the offense.

B. Use negative reinforcement tones.

C. You are **NEVER** out to **HURT**, but to **SHOCK!**

D. Use the Boomerang Technique – five times – **ONLY!**

E. Clear the dog's brain **BEFORE** an after-the-fact correction.

F. The dog **KNOWS** through the "**NOSE!**"

G. The **SOAKING-IN** period of time is at least 45 minutes.

H. Use your imagination – balloons, mousetraps, etc.

I. The formula for Extra Challenging Situations: 3 corrections a day for 3 days, every 3 hours.

J. The **LOVE** factor –
SHOCKLOVE! SHOCKLOVE! SHOCKLOVE!

"Z." The degree of the shock (the correction) must be commensurate with the degree of the offense, size and power of your dog; otherwise, your dog will just think of you as a ninny, and you will have to make your corrections 1000 times, 1001 times...!

YOU WILL NOT solve your dog's obnoxious, notorious and/or dangerous behaviors by kissing him behind the ear or giving him caviar. So ... the next time someone "OBJECTS" to the way that YOU correct YOUR dog, consider the "source" and remember my good friend, First Sergeant KIZER, U.S.M.C., a wise man – he is! He wore so many "distinguishing" ribbons on his chest that the weight of them made him walk at a slant – this man, without question "Walks-The-Walk and Talks-The-Talk." Just one of his many wisdoms: "THERE ARE NO CONSCIENTIOUS OBJECTORS 'ON' THE FIRING-LINE OR 'IN' FOX-HOLES."

When "he" knows that "he" knows, and "you" know that "he" knows, and "he" knows that "you" know "he" knows, but "he" chooses to disobey — there in lies the challenge! Make a correction — period!

"Dooowwwn!"

Diana and Rambo demonstrate Step "O."

LESSON #108
THE DOWN AND STAY COMMAND
THE SIT FROM THE DOWN COMMAND

THE DOWN AND STAY COMMAND

In many cases, the Down and Stay Command can be the hardest command to teach a dog. The reason is that to a dog it represents **total** submission, plus the fact that they **do not** like to lie down unless **they** have chosen the place to lie down. This tendency is inherent from their wild nature. When dogs are in the down position, they feel vulnerable because all their defenses **are** down. This is the reason why many animals of the wild, including the dog, when they lie down, always look for shelter, in a camouflaged area, a corner, or a cave, and always, when they go into the chosen spot, turn around, and lie down **facing** the territory in a position where **nothing** can get to them from the sides or the back.

Because of these tendencies, the Down and Stay Command **should not** be taught in any way, shape or form by forcing the dog. As a rule, the more you try to **force** them down, the more **they will resist.** The only way the Down and Stay Command should be taught is through the **natural** submissiveness of their nature. We **know** that the down position is the way that animals in the wild submit to one another or to a higher power; such as a runt submitting to a larger one of their kind or to the leader of the pack. You may have noticed that when two dogs are at hard play or in a fight, in most cases, sooner or later, one will "bow-down" to the other. They will lie down. They will **surrender!** So once again, keeping this in mind, teaching the Down and Stay Command should **only** be taught through the **natural** submissiveness of the dog. Think of it as between you and your dog: Who is bigger? Who stands taller? Who is the higher power? **Who is the leader?**

I consider the Down and Stay Command to be one of the most important commands that we can teach our dogs. Why? Because through it, for periods when we need **total** control, we can almost take "the dog" out of the dog.

Stanley's wife Maria told me that one day she started to take their Yellow Labrador, Sierra, for a walk. She only got as far as the sidewalk in front of their house when she heard their phone ring. She commanded Sierra to "Down and Stay," and ran into the house. "After my phone call, I got carried away with chores until about 2 1/2 hours later, when I remembered...Sierra! I ran to the front of the house only to find Sierra in the exact same spot. She had not moved an inch from where I had placed her. I was so proud of her!"

At the school for guide dogs, trainers create situations that will tempt the dogs to break whatever position we have placed them in. As we are running at heel with another dog, we'll jump over dogs in a down stay. We'll sail a frisbee just above their heads, or we play ball which we accidentally on purpose miss and let go flying into the dogs. The guide dog must hold position no matter what the circumstance. As I instruct the students, I instruct you! "If the guide dog can hold the down and stay position, no matter what the distraction, so...can...your...dog! Go for it!"

"HONEY!"

These two examples illustrate "DOWN" steps A through G.

"Dooowwwn!"

TRAINING

A. Teaching this command begins with the dog at the Sit at Heel position.

B. As when teaching the Sit and Stay Command, all rules related to **not** showing our insecurities, are also applicable to the teaching of this command, i.e. stand erect, do not lean over, do not waver, etc.

C. Hold the leash in your **left** hand to the point where when you hold your left hand **in front of you**, the leash dangles in the shape of a "U" between your left hand and the dog's neck. The bottom of the "U" should be at the level of the bottom of the dog's chest.

D. As you hold your left hand securely in front of you, place the ball of your left foot on the leash (the bottom of the "U" area) and **gently** lower the leash to the ground. The leash should now be **taut** between the dog's neck and the floor. The idea here is **not to force the dog down** but simply to hold him in position and to give **direction** to the desired result. Depending on your dog's size, you may have to adjust the level of the "U" section of the leash. **Remember – do not force the dog.**

E. Raise your right hand above your head in a "heil" manner, as you simultaneously call the dog's name. **Hold** that position for three seconds.

F. Smartly snap your right arm and hand in a downward and **forward** manner as you **simultaneously command,** "Dooowwwn!" Elongate the "o" and "w" for a more effective tone. Your right hand and arm should now be directly in front of you and parallel to the floor.

In performing this step, the tendency of many students is to slightly turn their bodies to the left (towards the dog) and, **unfairly**, snap the arm and hand above the dog's head. **DON'T!**

G. Hold the "D" position (as described on page 271), for as long as it takes, until the dog lowers his body to whatever extent. Some will readily go all the way down, others will hold for a long period, and others will drop just enough to loosen the leash between their neck and your foot. Remember what we are asking here goes **totally** against their nature. If necessary, give the hand signal and verbal command every 30 seconds. However, after holding your hand signal for 5 seconds, you may relax your hand and arm by lowering them to the side of your body.

H. If the dog drops just enough **to loosen** the leash, wait five seconds or so (make sure **at this time** that he is not going down all the way), then **retighten** the leash by raising your left hand, and again give your hand and arm signal with the verbal command. Repeat **this** step until the dog **does go all the way down.**

I. At whatever point the dog does go **all the way** down, **do not** do anything for five seconds. Make sure that he is **solidly** down, then **casually** tighten the leash under your foot and his neck to the point where if he tried to get up again, he couldn't. This teaches him that once he is down he is down "for the count." Once the dog is down, **he has to stay down,** until another command is given. Now, connect with your LOVE factor, "Good boy! Good boy!" and a slight pat on the head.

Placing and keeping your left foot on the leash close to the neck line when the dog is down is a very good way of controlling him, especially when you are in distractive situations, i.e. a crowd, lots of children or other dogs.

J. Hold the "I" position (as described above) for at least fifteen seconds, then **casually** remove your left foot from the leash. **The dog is now down on his own recognizance.** If he tries to get up, put your foot back on the leash. After he's been down **on his own recognizance** for about five seconds,

"Dooowwwn!"

Steps A through I demonstrated.

"Dooowwwn!"

Steps A through I demonstrated. Notice the
dog's "submissiveness" look on the drop.

adjust the leash to the heel position, and **smartly** stepping forward, give the Heel Command. As you step forward, **do not** give a jerk unless you absolutely have to – to whatever extent possible, let the dog perform on his own!

K. Take him for a **very short** walk, return to the same place where you were and do the maneuver again. Each time before doing this maneuver, you should first do a **short** walk.

L. Repeat the maneuver three times per session for two days; no more than three sessions per day.

M. After just a few sessions, you'll find that the dog will start dropping to the down position at the slightest snap of the signal or verbal command. You may now stop using the leash. When this is attained, give the Stay Command and start moving around your dog in a circle. The same as we did with the Sit and Stay Command.

N. After you can walk a complete circle around the dog clockwise and counter-clockwise, without him breaking position, step over him from his left to his right and visa versa. At first, **move slowly** as you simultaneously give the Stay Command. Then you can run and jump over him. An **important point to remember** whenever you go over him is to always step **first** with the foot **farthest** from his head, otherwise the maneuver is too vulnerable for him. It's as if you were going to **kick** his head.

"DOWN...STAY!"

Aimee and Ringo demonstrate Step N.

O. In time, you'll find that the dog will readily respond to either the verbal or hand signal. When this is accomplished, standing 6 – 8 feet away, start giving **only** the signal from the front of the dog. Do as follows:

1. Have the dog sit and stay.

2. Somewhere in front of the dog, stand 6–8 feet away.

3. Call the dog's name **only** if you need to get his attention – you may have to follow with a quick Stay Command.

4. Raise your hand and arm above your head and **smartly snap** your hand and arm in a downward manner. Your hand and arm should now be pointing towards the floor at his front paws. Hold this position for forty-five seconds. If the dog does not drop, firmly follow with the verbal command. If he still does not drop, you are in a **challenge** situation. See the example on page 266.

P. What to do in the challenge situation:

1. Return to the dog.

2. Hold the leash as explained in "C" on page 271.

3. Place your left foot on the "U" section of the leash, and in this case, **jerk** him down by **smartly shoving** your foot to the floor. **Before you do this, make sure that it is a challenge situation.** Remember the definition.

4. Do not forget the LOVE factor.

Courtney and Zoe demonstrate Step P, #3.
On the challenge, jerk him down!

"**Z.**" In increments of fifteen minutes per week, build the down and stay with your dog to a four hour period, or whatever lesser time you desire. The reason why it's important and we highly recommend teaching a **long down and stay** is that it has an effect on the entire dog. It **teaches him self-control** and, after all, is it not self-control that we want from our dogs? Self-control from jumping on people, chewing on your furniture, getting into the trash, etc.

When giving this direction, many students exclaim, "Dave, did you say **four hours?** Are you serious or are you crazy? Isn't that unfair to the dog?"

My reply is always, "I ask **you,** what does a guide dog for the blind do about 75% of the time? Picture him with the daily routine of his blind master. Think about it. What does **any** dog do on "their own" 90% of time? They are lying down aren't they? Therefore, if they can do it on their own, they can certainly do it on command! **And you should expect them to!**"

"On the other hand, be fair, don't expect your dog to lie there for four hours like a Marine at attention. **Do allow some basic movement,** i.e. to stretch, to chew on a rawhide, to get a drink of water, to go to sleep, or to simply just wiggle."

If your dog at any time during the training of the Down and Stay Command begins to emotionally "lose it"—vigorously fights your efforts—you may have to teach this command the **natural, natural, natural** way. The dogs to be especially careful with are the giant types—Rottweilers, St. Bernards, Great Danes, etc.—and the miniature types—Cairn Terriers, Pomeranians, Yorkshire Terriers, etc.

1. Immediately stop teaching the command as outlined.

2. Over emphasize the sit and stay, and then just wait. Give the command..."Dowwwwn"... and wait.

3. You will find that sooner or later, the dog will drop to the down position on his own. They all do, sooner or later—if you wait long enough.

4. As he is "dropping," you passively command, "Dowwwn...goooodboyyy...ssstaaay."

5. In your daily living with your dog repeat the command just as described above each time that you see him going to the lying down position on his own.

6. You will find that in time, sooner or later, he will respond to the down command...**on command!**

**IRENE TURGEON
ON "THE CHALLENGE!"**

"RAMBO!"

"Dowwwn!"

"Dowwwn!"

THE SIT FROM THE DOWN COMMAND

This is a kind of neat command and one that very few dogs in the world can do.

I like to encourage all of our students to definitely teach it to their dog, and I encourage **you** to do the same. The reason is two fold. Experience tells us that the more commands you teach and expect your dog to perform, the more overall control you have of him – **the more you are "The Leader of The Pack."** This is in contrast to the lifetime of **subservient signals** most of us humans give to our dogs when we literally **bow down** to them. Actions which the dog interprets as our paying homage to them – "Allah! Allah! Allah! Ali BaBa!"

Picture it: When we put on the collar or leash, brush or bathe them, whatever, and the dog, not wanting to submit, slinks down, rolls over, squirms, wiggles, or throws all fours up in the air. During this time we are bending over **(bowing down)**, attempting to accomplish our task.

Imagine a blind person having to go through all this nonsense with their guide dog. In contrast, the guide dog wears a harness that has attached to it an inverted "U" shaped handle. This is what the blind person holds on to and receives from his dog guiding signals. When the blind person puts the harness on his dog there is no battle. In most cases he simply holds the harness in front of his dog and the dog crawls into it. Some dogs, once in the harness, actually adjust their body to fit comfortably in it. The blind master has only to fasten the buckle under the dog and be on their merry way.

So don't spend your lifetime bowing down to your dog. At least have him meet you half-way by sitting. Follow the directions below to teach him the Sit from the Down Command.

TRAINING

A. With the dog in the down position, stand very erect in front of him approximately one foot away.

B. Hold your right arm and hand **straight** down, a little away from your body, palm **facing** the dog.

C. As you lift your hand and arm straight up in the air in a swooping way—just as if you were picking him up—give the command to "SSSSIT!" Make encouraging moves above his head (snap your fingers or clap your hands), and simultaneously give encouraging remarks, "Come on puppy, sit, sit!" Do this two or three times. You'll find that most dogs will readily come up to the sit or stand position. If they stand, you immediately command, "SIT!"

"SSSSIT!"

Genene and Rambo

D. Should your dog be one who does **not readily** come up to the sit position after giving the encouraging remarks and moves above his head, "accidentally on purpose" quickly and shockingly begin to step on his paw **(do not hurt him)**, and keep doing so **(crowd him, stay with it, don't let him win!)** until he does come up. When he does come up, connect with the LOVE factor, "GOOD BOY! GOOD BOY! SSSSIT! SSSSIT! SSSSTAY!"

With a little practice and follow through you only have to take a close step towards his paws as you give the signal or verbal command and he will readily respond.

E. When the dog is used to the verbal and signal commands and readily Sits from the Down Command, have him hold the position while you practice two or three times taking the collar and leash off and putting it back on. The dog must hold the sit position until you have **quickly** accomplished your task with him.

My dogs put on their own collars. As the blind master does with his guide dog, I just hold the collar open in front of them, and they slip their heads right in to it. Your dog will too – try it.

F. Never (unless you're in a mushy-loving-necking situation) **bow down** to your dog. Always have him meet you half way. Have him come up to the sit position and hold it until you **quickly** accomplish your task with him and give another command.

"Z." A Word of Caution: As mentioned, the Down and Stay Command can be a difficult one for many dogs to accept. For this reason, DO NOT, I repeat, DO NOT be in a hurry to teach the Sit from the Down Command. Before teaching this command be sure that at least two weeks have gone by since your dog learned to **readily** accept the Down and Stay Command. Otherwise you could create confusion and trauma in your dog which would hinder and delay not only these two commands, but the entire training process.

TID-BITS TO PONDER AND REMEMBER

A. Force will not do it – guidance will.

B. Especially when teaching the Down and Stay Command, do not lean over—have the dog submit to you, not you to him.

C. When giving the down signal, do not snap your arm and hand on top of the dog, instead they must be in front and away from the dog.

D. Definitely teach your dog The Sit from the Down Command.

"Z." Because of the importance and sensitiveness of teaching these two commands, I encourage you to carefully read this lesson at least twice. Pay close attention to all the steps before applying them to your dog.

THE COME COMMAND

The perfect Come Command.
He comes! Sits in front of you and looks squarely into your eyes!

LESSON #109
THE COME COMMAND

How many times have we seen people running after their dog and hollering, "Come! Come! Come!" And their dog is traveling 50 miles per hour in the opposite direction. "Why?"

The Come Command is a command that many people have trouble with. They tell me, "Dave, my dog can do everything. He'll sit, stay, down and stay, roll over, even stand on his ear, but **he will not come! Why?**"

There are many reasons for this. One of them is that **unknowingly** owners **teach** their dog **not** to come. Plus we humans assume that dogs perceive all things the same as we do, **but they don't.** We'll talk more about this later.

I've found that the main reason is the lack of a proper relationship between the master and the dog. The dog is not yet **fully** convinced that his master is indeed the leader of the pack. The dog's point of view is, "Hey, I'm off leash, so therefore if I don't obey, there-is-nothing-you-can-do-about-it!" So, until the dog responds to the Come Command, the person who tells me that his dog can do **everything,** really can't!

There are various reasons for dogs not responding to the Come Command, but they all take root with improper handling techniques, such as the "un-master" who will call the dog and on arrival slaps, kicks, or in some sundry way ridicules the dog. Given these circumstances, would **you** come?

Before you try the Come Command off-leash, make certain your dog can, without hesitation, respond to all the basic commands, including Come ON the leash.

An important factor to consider when teaching the Come Command is that when you call your dog from a distance, he basically **can not see you.** Why not? According to science, dogs are basically color blind and see only in shades of gray. When training guide dogs, many people ask, "How does the dog know to stop when the light is red, or go when it's green?" In either case the dog doesn't know, he doesn't even see the traffic signal. The **judgment** as to "go" or "not go" must be made by the blind master through his over-developed hearing, and the training provided to him at the school for guide dogs.

Because dogs lack color vision, they are also hampered in dimension. When we humans look at things, we look **directly** at them; we see the colors, shapes, and dimensions. At a distance, especially when the dog turns to look your way, he is looking at **everything** in a running sequence. He sees the big picture. For all you know, he thinks that you're a tree out there, or a...well...maybe not a fire hydrant! In any event, **he doesn't see you as you**. This isn't to say that they have **bad** vision. To the extent that they can see, they have very **good** vision; however, their vision requires **movement** – especially at a distance.

It's for this very reason that when calling your dog from a distance (especially when you're beginning the training), you should provide him with a signal – **a big moving signal – YOU!** Using your whole body, wave, moving from side to side with either one of your arms stretched above your head. Become a flag as you call his name. When you have his attention, give the verbal command, "COME! COME!" as you take two or three steps backwards. This mix of movements gives your dog something to **focus** on, something to **narrow down** on; then he knows exactly where to come. Remember that the dog does not have bad vision, they have dog vision.

The best way to parallel the nature of a dog's vision and the requirement of movement is to look at the following situation:

Say that with our dogs we're standing in the middle of an open field, like a football field, and about twenty feet away is a bunny rabbit. Now, I ask you, what does that bunny rabbit do to keep from being seen by the dog?...It's amazing how God takes care of all of us. But what happens if the bunny rabbit moves? Can you picture it? The-chase-is-on, isn't it. This is the way a dog's vision works. It's also been my experience that in many cases the dog sees more through his over-developed smell and hearing senses.

What is the most important rule when teaching the Come Command to your dog? Bar any other rule, **the most important** is that whenever you command your dog to come, wherever you are—at the beach, the park, the yard, the house, wherever—the maneuver is **not complete** until he has **come, sat and stayed in front of you for at least ten seconds.** The last part of the maneuver is to **praise him – lavishly!** Why are these last two steps so important? Without them, I'm convinced that this is where most people go wrong and end up teaching their dog **not** to come.

Think about it. How many times have you seen people or been guilty of it yourself, call the dog from wherever he is, "Hey Fido, where are you, come!" The dog comes running, but when he's half-way or thereabouts, the master spots him and says, " Oh, there you are, good boy! Good boy!" and goes back to whatever activity he was doing. The dog, having arrived half-way to his destination, stands puzzled, takes a couple of sniffs, turns around, and goes back to whatever **he** was doing. Beginning at puppyhood, we continuously do this to our dogs. Then the day arrives when you **really** want the dog to come. Forget it! Chances are you've cried "wolf" **once too many times.**

Again remember the Come Command is never over until the dog has sat and stayed for at least ten seconds in front of you. I gave these instructions to a Drill Instructor at the Marine Corp Recruit Depot in San Diego, and added, "If you can get him to **salute you** when he gets there, all the better!" He took this as a challenge and actually taught his Jack Russell Terrier, Terror, to paw-salute him every time he sits in front of him. It's certainly one of the cutest things I've seen. Terror actually raised his paw to his little head, which he slightly lowered. It resembled an exaggerated paw-shake. You may want to try this with your dog – it is very cute.

For better control, ease of training, and security, when teaching the Come Command use a 30 or 40 foot cotton webbed leash, sometimes known as a lunge line. Avoid the nylon type as they can be hard on your hands and they tangle too easily and lose their shape.

This lunge line leash is very good in training the Come Command. In addition, you'll find that in many situations throughout the life of your dog, it will be useful for total control and security. Just let him drag it, but **never** without supervision. Should he try to get away from you while on this leash, you can be sure that he won't get far before you can grab it or it tangles and he can't move. **Be careful that you don't get tangled into the leash, especially if you have a big dog!**

1. THE COME COMMAND

Diana and Rambo demonstrate the Come Command.

2. THE COME COMMAND

"Come! Come!"

"Ssssit!"

3. THE COME COMMAND

TRAINING

A. To begin teaching the Come Command, attach your long leash and place your dog at the sit-stay or down-stay position. During practice you should vary the position.

B. Firmly give your Stay Command and retreat to your desired distance. Start with six feet and increase it by five feet every couple of days. As you move away from him, walk **backwards** until you've reached your desired distance. At this point give your Stay Command again.

C. Pause for about fifteen seconds to a minute (vary the time during practice). Then with your arm stretched like you're reaching for the sky, wave it along with your body, as you call your dog's name in a friendly but firm tone, "PRINCE! PRINCE!" Now that you have his attention, give the command twice, as you take two or three steps backwards, "COME! COME!"

D. If the dog gives any signs of wanting to come, immediately go to praise tones, "GOOD BOY! GOOD BOY!" and as he's coming say, "COME, COME!"

E. When he reaches the distance of about three feet from you, pointing your palm towards him, begin giving the command, "SSSSIT! SSSSIT!" By doing this, you'll find that he will kind of slide into the position, especially when he's running from a distance. But no matter what, even if **you** have to adjust yourself, end the maneuver with the dog sitting in front of you before praising him. If he tries to side-step you, move over and block him.

F. After he has sat in front of you, pause for about ten seconds. This makes him **solid** in the position. After these ten seconds, go to your LOVE factor in a very **lavish** way. **This position and period of time are very important** because they'll keep your dog on the **alert** for another command or release. You'll find that in time, he'll come and sit and look at you squarely in the eyes.

G. If the dog doesn't come after the first call, try again two more times, making certain that you wait about fifteen seconds between each call. If he still doesn't come after the third call, pick up the leash and give a couple of **encouraging** jerks towards you. If you must, reel him in, but only to the extent necessary.

H. When the dog comes, before you make any self-adjustments or corrections, always give the dog the benefit of the doubt and allow him to perform **on his own**. This holds true whether he's on a loose leash or off-leash.

I. Always end the maneuver with the dog sitting in

front of you, and always with **lavish** praise after he has sat in front of you for ten seconds.

J. Repeat this procedure five times during each training session. You'll find that before long (most dogs do it within the first three sessions,) you will only have to **wave** and the dog will come running!

K. Some dogs will **jump-the-gun** and come running to you the moment you have reached a **certain** distance. To avoid this, vary the times and distance that you are away before you call. On occasion instead of calling him, go all the way back to him. Vary the maneuvers. Avoid patterns that will only confuse your dog.

"Z." To solidify the Come Command, do the following trick: **Caution:** Before you do it, you must make sure that your dog, **without a doubt,** knows exactly what **come** means.

1. Gather a couple stones. I don't mean boulders – I also don't mean pebbles. **Use appropriate judgement.** The stone size should be correspondent to your dog's size.

2. In an open space or field (your back yard, if it's big enough), turn your dog loose, or have him on the long leash. Have him move about 25 feet away from you. Don't

coax him, have him move away on his own. When he's distracted, "locked on a sniff" or whatever, call him in a **low, passive, non-authoritative manner**. The tone should be just audible enough for him to hear you. Because you called in this passive manner, the chances of him coming are remote. Wait for five seconds or so, and call again. This time your tone is a little stronger, but **still passive**. Wait another five seconds or so. Then if he doesn't come, without him seeing you throw it, **blast** him with one of the stones that you set yourself up with.

3. When the dog isn't looking, throw the stone to hit hard. You're not going to hurt him. However, the **rump** should be the area that you're aiming for. When the stone hits (this will be a **shock** to him), he'll turn around to look your way. When he does, you should, as you wave your signal, sternly command, "COME! COME!" The second stone is in case you miss with the first one.

This method is part of the Boomerang Technique. However, in this case, the dog can not directly relate the stone to you. **Remember, he should not see you throw it!** Done correctly two or three times, this trick will definitely solidify the Come Command. You see, the dog has no knowledge of the stone. All the dog knows is that through some **voodoo** power that you have over him, **you can and will reach him.** Use this trick for all that it is worth.

Genene and Rudy also demonstrate the Come Command.

1. THE COME COMMAND

"Come!"

"Come!"

2. THE COME COMMAND

3. THE COME COMMAND

"Ssssit!"

ON THE CHALLENGE

A. Once you're convinced that the dog **definitely** knows what "Come!" means, and he doesn't come, consider this a **challenge**, stop calling "Come!" For you see, this is another way in which we humans teach our dogs **not to come** from the time that they were puppies.

Picture we humans with our puppy from the time he is eight weeks and older. We turn him loose, and he begins to stray and run. We holler, "COME! COME!" and he just

picks-up speed. He doesn't know "come" from "Adam!"
And we continue to holler, "Come! Come!" Now he looks
like a torpedo going away from us! The puppy continues to
grow. Now he's five-months-old, and we humans are still
hollering, "Come! Come!" What do you suppose he is going to do? He is going to **challenge** the situation,
and...run...run...run!

B. On the challenge, stop calling "come." Do not give
chase, don't get excited – don't make it a game for him. Use
your stone trick, or as best as you can, go to him, even if
you have to walk a mile. When you manage to nab the
culprit, put him on-leash and **immediately** jerk him all the
way to where you called him from – **all the way back to
home-base.** Remember that a jerk is not a pull. If, on the
way, he doesn't yelp a couple of times when you jerk him,
you're not being as effective as you could be. Also remember that this **is not** being unkind, for **this command** could
some day **save** your dog's life. I am talking from experience!

When I was about 13-years-old, I lost my 3-year-old Rusty
after he was run over by a car right in front of me. Rusty
died in my arms...and I will never forget it. My Rusty! He
was cuter than a punkin', and he died because he didn't
respond to the Come Command. **It was not his fault!**

"**Z.**" End the maneuver with him sitting in front of you for no less than ten seconds. Don't forget your passive LOVE factor. Repeat this procedure with every **challenge** situation, and watch it perform **magic** for you! Make the **investment of effort**, it will pay you **great dividends**.

Don't do as Deborah, as she smiled, suggested: "If Sumo doesn't come, Dave, you mean I can't use my back-up call? – Cooookie!"

A tip from Pam Strong, a veterinarian office manager: "I have always taught my dogs to 'look-out' for me rather than me looking-out for them. I play hide-and-seek with them, so when I say 'COME,' my dogs are always there."

Don't be like one of the owners that Naomi, an emergency clinic veterinarian technician in San Diego, sadly talks of, "I can't tell you how many dead puppies I have seen... and their hysterical owners."

Don't make "excuses" for your dog. **Solidly ... teach ... the come command!**

TID-BITS TO PONDER AND REMEMBER

A. Never, in any way, shape, or form, ridicule your dog after he has come to you.

B. Remember that a dog has "dog vision," therefore, motion is necessary.

C. "Come" means all the way to you each and every time.

D. When using the lunge line, don't put yourself in harms-way.

E. A stone does not mean a boulder, nor does it mean a pebble.

"Z." End the maneuver with lavish praise each and every time your dog comes.

THE ADVANCED LESSONS

SERIES #200

You can see your dog...

...but he can not see you!

LESSON #201
THE UNSUPERVISED STAY COMMAND –
MASTER OUT-OF-SIGHT

If only I had a dollar for every time that I've heard this complaint, "My dog will 'stay' as long as I'm right there with him, but no sooner do I turn my back..."

Prince and Honey are two of my German Shepherds. Prince is the oldest. All of their lives they have both loved to chase kitty-cats. Honey is the worst. In my travels they always go with me and on many occasions while I give my lessons they have to stay unsupervised in the wagon. Some lessons last up to two hours and because many times the weather is warm I have to leave all the windows to the station wagon down.

Picture this scenario: While Prince and Honey are waiting in the station wagon, a kitty-cat comes strolling by. Honey scrambles up to the rear window and says, "Prince! Prince! Look over there, let's go get him!" Prince scrambles to join Honey, but because he is "older and wiser," says to her, "Wait a minute, Honey, maybe we better not, because just as sure as we put one foot out the window, 'ole 'you-know-who' is going to show up and we'll get it!" It is precisely that thought that keeps Prince and Honey in the unsupervised stay position no matter where I am or how long I'm gone. It is precisely that thought that will keep your dog in the unsupervised stay position – with you out-of-sight.

TRAINING

A. Choose the **right training place**. One of the **best places** to train the Unsupervised Stay – with you out-of-sight – Command is in front of your house; especially if you have a peep hole in your front door, but a side window will do. The point is to position yourself where **you** can see the dog, but he can not see you. You don't have to see the whole dog, just a foot or tail is enough.

B. Attach your lunge line (the long leash—you can also use a clothes line—see page 293) to the dog and place him about twelve feet away from the front of your front door in the down and stay position.

C. Bringing the end of the lunge line with you, go to the front door, before you enter and close the door, turn to him and firmly command, "STAY!" At all times the end of the lunge line is in your hand. The rest of the line trails **loosely** between the dog and the front door.

D. Enter and close the door behind you. After no more than three seconds, turn and emphatically—shockingly—open the door. If the dog has already broken, go to him and emphatically shove him to the down position, as you firmly command, "YOU STAY!" and in a lower tone, "Now you be a good boy. You stay!"

Repeat the three second process. If this time the dog has remained in the down position, do not go to him, but from the front door exclaim, "YOU STAY. GOOD BOY. YOU STAY!" Do this procedure until you can go in and out of your front door three times. The dog may not break the down position. The period of time that you stay out-of-sight is built in increments of three seconds. The first time, three seconds; the second time, six seconds; the third time, nine seconds.

E. Now you are ready for the acid test. You are on the fourth round. The last words to the dog were, "You stay. Good boy. You stay!" After closing the door, from your vantage point, keep track of your dog and **wait. During this wait period,** especially during the beginning of training, it's only fair to the dog to **maintain silence.**

F. No matter how long you have to wait...**wait!** Keep your eye on him. He'll break soon enough. The **moment** that he does **break**, even if he just sits up, you bang the door, open it, and like gangbusters, run to him, grab him and in the same place where you had him, shove him down, as you sternly command, "NOW YOU STAY THERE. STAY!" And again, in a lower tone, "Now you be a good boy. Be a good boy! Stay!" The entire experience should be so shocking to him that he never again wants to break, unless you command him to do so.

G. Repeat the procedure. If the dog holds for three minutes, casually open the front door, go to him and lavishly praise him.

H. After you can get the dog to hold his position for three minutes, go for longer periods of time. You should now change the position where you will "show" (appear) from. The garage area or the side of the house are good spots. In any event, remember that the "wait and show from" place should be one where you can see the dog, but he can't see you. The more areas that you can show up from the better. Use your imagination. What you want to instill in the dog is that he feels like, **"He is (meaning you) everywhere! He's everywhere!"** and what causes you to "show" is his breaking position.

"**Z.**" To make your dog **solid** in this maneuver, you can set him up by having a friend (a stranger to the dog,) casually be passing by and attempt to call him off. If the dog breaks, follow through with your correction, and this time because he obeyed a stranger, show no mercy in your disapproval. This will help make him "**theft proof.**"

TID-BITS TO PONDER AND REMEMBER

A. Bear in mind that the Unsupervised Stay Command is an **advanced lesson. Before attempting to teach it, the dog should know that you are the leader of the pack!**

B. When you show yourself to the dog, it must appear like gangbusters. You must get through to him that **you are very upset.**

C. Vary the areas where you show from. When the dog understands what is expected of him, train him in various other locations, i.e., the bathroom at the park, your local convenience store, etc.

"**Z.**" When you show and the dog has not broken position, **the LOVE factor is emphatically in order!**

A FINAL WORD

This lesson could just as easily be called: "Controlling The Dog's Behavior While You're Away from Home, or Automobile." Think about it. See Lesson 107.

**STAY! IN AUTO.
MASTER OUT-OF-SIGHT!**

Dogs do not learn by osmosis; there are no two ways about it, you have to teach and practice with them. Practice! Practice! Practice! Practice does make perfect! Practice!

Happiness is... **A Better Canine!**

THE GO TO YOUR PLACE COMMAND

Scout, Jessie and Rumor

LESSON #202
THE GO TO YOUR PLACE OR
OUTSIDE COMMAND

This is a command that we urge **all** of our students to definitely teach to their dogs. "Why?" you may ask!

The usual span of life for a dog is ten to fifteen years. During this period, there will probably be many times **when you just don't want your dog in the way**; company arrives, or you're having a meeting, or somebody is ill. Look...**you** love your dog very much. **You do!** Unfortunately, not everybody else does! **And this is the truth of the matter – you love him, but not everybody else does.** Others may like your dog, but they do not love him like you do. How many times have you been to someone's home and their dog was all over you, licking and sniffing you. Did you like it?

In the interest of all concerned, the Go to Your Place or Outside Command is one that all dogs should be taught. On this verbal and/or signal command, the dog should **immediately** depart the premises and virtually disappear to a pre-designated place and stay there until released, or they should go outside. The signal is your outstretched arm and hand pointing towards the designated place.

DIANA AND RAMBO

1. "Go! Outside!"

2. "Do I really have to?"

3. "Yes, you have to! Go!"

TRAINING

A. Before you start, be sure that the dog has been taught Lesson 201, The Unsupervised Stay Command.

B. Determine where the dog's **out of the way** designated place is going to be. The place you choose should preferably be a place that the dog has already chosen on his own. Most dogs usually pick a couple of places within the home where they like to lie. If one of these places is acceptable to you, you're ahead of the game, as it will be easier to teach him this command.

C. Once you have determined the designated place, **on leash**, take the dog to the **farthest** point that you can get from the designated place, and still be within the confines (home or yard) of this designated area. At this farthest point, as you emphatically, with your arm extended, point towards the designated place, also emphatically command, "PLACE!" or, "PRINCE, PLACE!" Give the command three times in a row, with five second intervals: "PRINCE, PLACE!" ..."PLACE!" ..."PLACE!" Prince may look at you as if to say, "**Now**, what does he want from me!" (It's a new tone, and a new signal!)

D. After giving your command, quickly walk towards the place , as you periodically command, "Place!"

"Place!" "Place!" Keep the leash **loose.**

E. On arrival at THE PLACE, you may have to maneuver him a little, as you do so, command "PLACE!" then command, "DOWN!" "STAY!" "GOOD BOY!" After five minutes or so, call him off HIS PLACE, and upon his arrival to you, emphatically praise him.

F. Repeat the procedure as outlined, three times a day for three days.

G. At the end of three days, you can be sure that the dog basically knows the Place Command. On the fourth, fifth and sixth days of practice, **do not accompany** him all the way to The Place, instead in a casual way, **you stop three feet** from The Place (be sure to keep hold of **only** the **leash handle**). You'll find that the forward motion of your speedy walk towards The Place will carry the dog the remaining three feet. If it is necessary, shoo him into His Place.

H. Repeat step "G" three times a day for three days. Thereafter, **every three days back off your stopping point** by three feet (i.e., three feet, six feet, nine feet, and so on) until the dog can travel on his own from the original starting point to His Place.

I. After the first three feet that the dog travels on his own, no longer hold the leash, but casually drop it and let him drag it to His Place.

J. On the challenge: When your dog can travel the full distance, you can be sure that he knows The Go to Your Place Command from anywhere. Therefore, if he chooses to challenge you, settle the issue by jerking him all the way to His Place and subsequently have him perform the maneuver three times **without fault.**

"Go! Outside!"

"Z." Follow these same instructions for the Go Outside Command.

TID-BITS TO PONDER AND REMEMBER

A. Again, we urge you, **do teach** this command to your dog. If you follow the steps as outlined, **he will readily catch-on!**

B. Others may like your dog, but they do not love him...like you do!

"Z." I have often heard it said that, Beagles are not supposed to be trainable. You may also have heard this. This is not so! They may be hardheads, but they can be trained. Take Tarzan, a notorious Beagle who lives in La Jolla, California. In twenty minutes I taught him to go to his place. On his own, after giving the command, he travels a good forty feet – right to His Place! If Tarzan can do it...so can your dog!

SIT AND STAY IN BACK SEAT - PASSENGER SIDE

Note where dog is seated and
the position of the wedged leash in the rear door.

LESSON #203
AUTOMOBILE RIDING TECHNIQUES
YOU DON'T DESERVE A "WRRRUF" RIDE FROM YOUR DOG!

Training automobile riding techniques to guide dogs is very important. The same methods could be just as important for you and your dog.

How many times have we heard of uncontrolled dogs that were maimed or killed because they jumped out of the car into the path of another. Then there are the accidents that occurred because; "My dog jumped into my arms." or "My dog jumped from the back seat to the front, and it caused me to lose control of the car." or "My dog crawled under my feet and I couldn't put the brakes on." The dog should **never** be able to reach the driver.

There will be times when children, or items that you're carrying, need to be placed in the car before the dog is allowed in. You don't want him to jump in and act like a hooligan!

Prior to starting lessons at the school, we have the prospective students come to the school for a demonstration of our work. "Do we have to bring the dog?" many of the students ask, "We can't handle him in the car, he's a maniac!"

TRAINING

A. Before the dog is allowed to enter the automobile he should be taught to sit and stay by the **rear wheel** of the **passenger side** of the automobile.

B. The dog should enter **only** on the command IN or JUMP-IN!

C. His position is the sit and stay or down and stay in the right rear section of the automobile. Exceptions to this should be made **only** when you choose to allow them. However, he should **instantaneously** return to position on command! See examples on pages 322, 326 and 329.

D. In order to control the dog at the beginning of training, keep the leash on him.

1. Command IN or JUMP-IN!

2. Place the dog in the position explained in step "C."

3. From the dog's neck stretch the leash to the frame of the car's door and add two inches. At this point on the leash tie a knot and hold the knot just outside the door frame. Making certain to keep the leash from the door's mechanism, close the door on the leash with the knot just outside of the frame. This will restrain the dog in position. The knot on the leash keeps it from running through the door and lengthening.

You can thread the part of the leash that is outside through the window and into the car; or if it's long enough, loosely tie it down to the door handle. Another alternative is, before closing the door, hold only the knot just outside the door's frame, and as best you can, maneuver the rest of the leash into the car. Then quickly close the door so the leash doesn't slip out. With a little effort and practice, you'll find the best routine for you and soon it will be second nature. CAUTION: This alternative method should not be used if the car doors are made out of fiber glass or other sensitive materials. I learned this very expensive lesson the hard way.

If the dog is in his position—sit and stay or down and stay in the right rear section of the car—and can still reach the driver, shorten the leash between his neck and door frame, and change the position of the knot.

4. Should the dog struggle – **let him!** He will quickly

Measure the distance from the dog's neck to the door frame,
and add two inches.

realize that his struggle is to no avail and will settle down. In
time, you'll find him readily accepting his position, obeying
your command, and restraining him with the leash will **no
longer be necessary**, however the leash can also serve as a
"seat-belt."

E. On arrival to your destination, it should not be the
dog's prerogative to jump out when you open the door; he

should **step out,** and do so only on your command OUT. Once out, he should be taught to routinely sit and stay until another command is given. **This simple routine could some day save his life!** Controlling the dog at this juncture should be very easy for you because the leash is accessible to you **before** you open the door.

F. Should the dog break his stay position when entering or leaving the automobile (try to jump in or out,) **shock** him by tapping him with the door. Remember your LOVE factor!

G. To obtain a **solid** down and stay position once the dog is in the car, begin driving at 25 to 30 MPH. Keep your eye on him through the rear view mirror and when he breaks his position, immediately apply the brakes – **hard!** Make the rear of that car seem like a milk-shake to him. If he slams into the back of the front seat, don't worry about it. Turn to him and firmly command, "YOU SSSSSIT AND SSSSSTAY! NOW YOU BE A GOOD BOY!"

What you have imprinted into his brain is that this-not-so-pleasant-shock that he has experienced was caused by **his** moving from position. I've found that even with the wildest of dogs, the maneuver will not have to be repeated too many times if done correctly the first time!

For obvious reasons, when applying this technique, CAUTION should be used regarding the speed of travel, degree of braking, and the traffic around you. You should choose an isolated area, void of traffic.

This same technique can be used to teach your dog how to ride in the back of a van or truck. Although when riding in the back of a truck, a harness, which is designated for this purpose should also be used. Some municipalities now require this by law.

H. When you need to leave your dog in the car, be aware of **heat conditions** which could be **fatal** to your dog. Use judgment as to the length of time you leave him in the car. Some municipalities have laws which bar leaving a dog in the car. Never leave your dog in the car without the windows rolled down. (If you are using the leash to restrain your dog, open the window to the door that he is restrained to – but not more than 2 inches. You do not want to hang your dog.) In warm weather a good rule to follow is to **always leave all windows one third open.** In hot weather – leave the dog at home!

I. Should your dog be one that **barks** or tries to **jump out** while you're away, use the boomerangs to shock him. Use them in the same methods as described in Lesson 201, The Unsupervised Stay Command – Master Out of Sight."

"Z." Guide dogs for the blind are routinely taught to ride on the floorboard on the front passenger side, or the rear section of the automobile, between the master's legs. You'll be amazed at how readily most dogs can accommodate themselves to very small places.

A very happy Prince, my loyal and beautiful German Shepherd, once rode from Columbus, Ohio to Miami, Florida on the floorboard. We had no choice, there were a total of six adult passengers in the car. **Did Prince mind it? Not a bit! He loved it!** How do I know? He told me so – that's how I know!

Tie a knot on the leash, hold the knot outside the door
and close the door.

If you are a passenger, the following is a useful technique.

A. After the front (or back) door is opened, the dog is taught to sit and stay outside the automobile.

B. While holding **only** the handle of the leash, the master goes in first and the dog follows on the command IN.

C. The dog sits or lies in front, or between the master's legs.

D. The master checks to make sure that the dog's tail is fully in **before** closing the door.

E. On arrival, the dog goes out **first** and immediately sits and stays. The master follows.

F. If you use this technique and your dog is squirrely while in the car:

1. **Lower** the leash (approximately the center section) to the floorboard.

2. Place the **ball** of your foot on the leash.

3. With both hands, **pull** the leash to the point where

the dog is restrained between his neck, your foot and floor-board.

4. While riding, **loosen the leash a little**, but **be ready** to tighten again, if necessary.

5. You can also use this method to control your dog in any other close quarter situation.

THREE MAIN COMPLAINTS ABOUT DOGS AND THE AUTOMOBILE

A. "In the car, he acts like a wild hooligan."
This was covered at the beginning of the chapter.

B. "He gets sick and throws-up every time."

Many young dogs experience this and in most cases it's nothing to cause alarm. It's simply a matter of their not as yet having their "sea legs," which they are sure to obtain with a little experience and time. In most cases you can help by exposing the dog to the automobile in small, common-sense steps:

1. For a few days "visit" with him in the car with all doors and windows open and certainly **no movement** of the car.

2. For a few more days, close the doors, but not the windows.

3. For another few days, follow the instructions at the beginning of the chapter and take him for a ride just around the block and immediately on return, let him out of the car, praise him a little, turn him loose in his area, and ignore him for a while.

Each day, little by little, increase the length of the ride. In most cases, you'll find that the dog will quickly get used to riding – without becoming sick. If your dog continuous to get sick, check with your veterinarian.

C. "Trying, or getting him into the car, is an exhausting major battle."

One of the main reasons why dogs rebel at getting into the car is that somewhere in their youth, it traumatized them. This is also true of dogs that refuse to jump into the back of a pick-up truck. How many times have you seen people trying to get their dogs into an automobile or pick-up truck. They shove, and scream, and push, and pull; and the more they shove, and scream, and push, and pull – the more the dog resists. I walk up and say, "Whoa! Whoa! Let me help you." I then instruct them as follows:

1. **Never** try to **push or pull** the dog into doing any-thing. For you can be sure that they will **always resist**. First, open the door which the dog will jump through. Give as ample a berth as possible; don't expect the dog to squeeze in. If your car is a two door, move the back of the front seat—if not the entire seat—forward (especially at first.)

2. Settle the dog outside of the car. You may have to give a few jerks, but do not let the leash tighten. The leash must remain loose at all times. At this time, forget the rule about having your dog sit prior to getting into the automobile. Your only objectives at this moment are: 1) To have the dog settle, and 2) On a totally loose leash, have the dog go into the car **on his own**. Once the dog has settled, give lots of encouragement to draw him into the car. You may also have another person on the other side of the car holding the leash and also coaxing. Do whatever you have to do to get him to go into the car **on his own.** Drawing him with a tid-bit is a good way. In many cases I've seen a quarter of a "trained hot dog" work wonders! **Remember not to shove or push.** Keep the leash loose and have the dog go into the car on his own.

3. Once in, give him lots of love. In the majority of cases that I've personally worked with, the dog readily responds and becomes accustomed to the maneuver. However, **if all fails,** place both hands at the same point of a short (one

foot) leash and give a jerk that is so swift that it propels the dog into the car before he even knows what happened. You can also pick him up and put him into the car in rapid-fire order – do not dilly-dally. Once in, give him lots of love.

This last technique is the same that we use in teaching a guide dog for the blind to ride on an escalator. Picture it. What dog would not, at first, shy away from the shaking and rumbling of an escalator? If we trainers were to push and pull the dog, we would never get them on the escalator. What do we do instead?

a. We expose the dog to the escalator, and give lots of praise and reassurance.

b. The moment the dog begins to shy away from it, we swiftly jerk him onto the escalator.

c. Once on, we give the dog lots of love. We pat the sides of the escalator to assure him that there is nothing to fear. Before long, the dog without hesitating, happily steps on...on command!

4. When teaching the dog to jump onto the back of a truck, use the same techniques as explained for a car, but first back the truck into a sidewalk or other higher ground, making the floor of the truck as level to the ground as

possible. Begin with as low a step as possible. You can then gradually increase the size of the jump and have the dog readily accept it with pleasure. Do not push and do not shove. **Use lots of common-sense, and remember that with anything that is taught, one grain at a time will move a mountain.**

TID-BITS TO PONDER AND REMEMBER

A. The dog should never be able to reach the driver.

B. Do not put your dog – or yourself – in harm's way.

"Z." **Never** push or pull your dog into doing anything – do not dilly-dally, get the **action** habit.

In my travels to and from students' homes to give lessons, my Prince, Honey and Rambo always ride with me. Because they are in the station wagon so much of the time, I allow them at all times to move freely about the full length of the rear compartment. They have become so good at my need for additional visibility in heavy traffic or changing lanes, that on my command, DOWN! they **immediately** drop. Sometimes all I have to do is look over my shoulder. Other times, they just hear the ticking of the turn signal and they immediately drop. To release them back into free movement, I simply command, "OOOkay, gooood puppies! Good boy, Prince. Good boy, Rambo! Good girl, Honey!" It always pleases me so to see their happy responses and wiggles, the way they jump up from position, and the way they go around and around. They often remind me of little fish in a bowl.

Prince, Honey and Rambo have become excellent travelers. So can: Fido, Widget, Rufus, Boomer, Jo Jo, Raisin, Rover, and...Zimba!

RAMBO GOES HOLLYWOOD!

Note The "Shades!"

A FINAL WORD

CAUTION: Do not put the dog in harm's way when using the leash-wedged-in-the-door method.

Note that in all the examples (pages 322, 326 and 329) the window on the side where the dog is positioned is open but only to the extent that the dog cannot jump out. You do not want to "hang" your dog.

A. "HALT! HALT!" B. "DOWN!"

C. "STAY!"

LESSON #204
THE HALT COMMAND

The Halt Command is an advanced lesson and should be taught only after the basics have been mastered. It is essential, especially if your dog is overly protective or you are going to train your dog in protection techniques, that he should be taught the Halt Command. On this command, no matter what the dog is doing, he should stop **dead in his tracks**. He should drop to the down position and stay until another command is given.

This command is also useful in runaway situations, or keeping your dog from entering into dangerous territory.

When teaching the Halt Command, the only equipment needed is an item that you can easily and accurately throw from a distance. A small bag full of sand, or beans, or a metal slip-chain will do. In this instance, we'll call this item your boomerang, but **do not use the actual boomerangs** (described in Lesson 107) which are used only for problem solving and teaching boundary limits.

A. "HALT! HALT!"   B. "DOWN!"

C. "STAY!"

TRAINING
TID-BITS TO PONDER AND REMEMBER

A. In an open but secure area, place the dog in the down and stay position.

B. Leave the dog in the stay position and move approximately fifty feet away from him.

C. Call your dog, and when he is approximately **one fourth** of the distance to you, with your arms outstretched towards him, **lunge forward** as you emphatically and excitedly command, HALT! HALT! You'll find that his tendency will be to slow down, if not totally come to a halt.

D. If the dog does HALT, immediately follow with DOWN! DOWN! and then...STAY!

E. If the dog does not halt immediately, throw your boomerangs (remember not the ones described in Lesson 107) right at his paws. I've used a handful of ordinary rocks or heavy gravel, and most of the time, this will halt him.

F. When you have gotten the dog to halt, down and stay, go to him and praise him, but do not be so lavish that it would cause him to break his position.

G. Have the dog stay and you return to the place where you originally called him from.

H. Call the dog and this time have him come all the way to you, where you should be emphatic with your praise.

I. Repeat steps A through H three to five times each session. Every second, third or fourth time that you call, **do not** halt the dog, instead have him come all the way to you. In other words, vary your commands. If you halt the dog too many times in a row, you will mix him up and nullify the Come Command. The dog's tendency would be to stop halfway every time you gave the Come Command.

"Z." On the Challenge

Once your dog has learned the Halt Command, practice it in various situations. Have him chase a ball or a frisbee, or some other unexpected situation, give the command. If he does not "stop-on-a-dime-and-get-nine-cents-change," go to him, leash him, and jerk him all the way to where he should have halted. Place him, and you return to where you originally gave the command. Call him and on his arrival praise him. Have him perform the command at least twice without fault before releasing him to his own recognizance.

The map is not always the territory. **You** are the one on the firing line; **you** are the one who knows your dog; **you** are the one who knows yourself. Read this book from cover to cover and do **your** very best.

Happiness is... **A B**etter Canine!

He may move about the area...

...but he can not cross the boundary line.

LESSON #205
BOUNDARY LIMIT TECHNIQUES

In Lesson 109, The Come Command, I shared the loss of my boy, Rusty to a speeding automobile. Rusty and I were playing in the front yard, my mother and brothers were also there. My younger sister was across the street coming home when Rusty spotted her and gave chase. Rusty died in my arms. Rusty did not respond to the Come Command, and he did not know his boundaries.

All dogs should be taught their **safe boundary limits.** The dog can cross that line **only** on command or on leash. Boundary limit techniques don't have to apply only to street situations. They can also be applied to areas within the home, such as the kitchen or dining room, or a living room you reserve for guests – any area you want the dog to be in, only when he has been invited.

Boundary training is an advanced lesson. Before teaching it, be sure that your dog knows the basic commands very well. It's easier to teach the dog his boundaries if he has been taught the Halt Command. The equipment needed is a 15 to 30 foot lunge line and six boomerangs (see Lesson 107). For better monitoring of the dog, it is recommended that two persons apply this training.

TRAINING

A. First determine the boundary limits. These should be as clear as possible to the dog. For example, the end of a grass line, a row of hedges, the line following a retaining wall. If a clear line is not available an imaginary line can be drawn.

B. Attach the 15 to 30 foot lunge line to the dog and let him drag it **within** the boundary zone.

C. Should the dog break on you—starts running and crosses the boundary line— you can readily grab the end of the lunge line and correct him by jerking him back inside the boundary line. If he actually gets away from you, you can be sure that he will not get far – the lunge line will easily hook around an object in the area, such as a bush or automobile tire, and bring him to a halt. Then, make your corrections.

D. With the lunge line still on, turn the dog loose within the boundary zone and mill about. At this time have the boomerangs with you – three on each person (remember it's easier to do this with two people). The dog should not be aware of them! So, as much as possible, keep from rattling them. It's also important not to say anything to the dog as you are milling about.

E. Start quickly walking towards the outside of the boundary line. In most cases, the dog will follow. If the dog does not follow, try again... mill about and head out again.

F. When the dog does follow, and you are approximately 3 feet from the boundary line, **as you are walking**, using your hand signal, command him to STAY!

G. When the dog sees your continued forward motion, his tendency will be to momentarily stop and quickly draw towards you again.

H. You are now ahead of him and **outside** the boundary line. It's important that you continue walking forward. Keep your eye on the dog and the moment that he starts to cross the boundary line, you **blast** him with the boomerangs as you command "GET BACK!" Be sure, however, that you are throwing the boomerangs right at the dog's paws and **on the boundary line.** The dog's tendency will be to repel farther **within** the boundary zone; if he doesn't, keep throwing until he does.

I. Now **YOU are OUTSIDE and HE is INSIDE** the boundary. Mill about – run, sing a song, throw a frisbee, whatever. **Short of calling the dog**, do whatever necessary to tempt him to **draw** towards you and outside the boundary line. If he does draw, throw your boomerangs again. At first your milling about **outside** of the boundary line should be no more than three minutes.

J. After three minutes, head for the **inside** of the boundary, cross it and stop with your heels right **on** the line.

K. Again, short of calling the dog, draw him to the line using exuberant praise. "Good Boy! Good Boy!" When he gets there, be lavish in your praise, but do not let him cross the line.

L. After thirty seconds or so of praise at the line, **without** saying anything further to the dog, once again mill about **inside** the boundary area.

M. Repeat procedures A through K, but this time **do not** give the command to stay as you approach the boundary line. The dog's tendency will be to stop or hesitate where he was boomeranged, if he doesn't, throw the boomerangs again.

N. Do this procedure for three days at the various lines you don't want him to cross. Thereafter, put him to the test once a week for a month.

O. To reinforce the boundary lines, you may set the dog up to draw him towards the line while you are **inside** the boundary. If he draws near the lines, throw your boomerang **over** his head and **on the line while** commanding, GET BACK OVER HERE!

P. On each boundary line where you trained (boomeranged) the dog, he will more or less recognize this boundary **up to 25 feet** in each direction.

Q. Once your dog understands his boundaries, he should be permitted to cross them only **on leash** or **on command.**

"Z." On the challenge:

Should your dog break his boundaries, **do not call him,** instead **go after him.** When you nab the culprit, snap the leash on him and **jerk** (don't pull – but **jerk**) him **all the way** to the point where he broke. When you get there, straddle the line and give him one final heavy-duty jerk that propels him back into his boundaries. Proceed by negatively reinforcing his staying within his boundaries by grabbing a short leash and **momentarily** pulling (not jerking) him, towards the outside of the boundary, as you **negatively** and **emphatically** command, DO YOU WANT

TO GO OUT THERE AGAIN! DO YOU! DO YOU!
You will find that his tendency will be to repel, to pull away
from the line. As he does so, quickly release the leash, which
will cause him to somewhat loose his footing backwards.
Command, NOW YOU GET BACK IN THERE AND
BE A GOOD PUPPY!

TID-BITS TO PONDER AND REMEMBER

A. Before teaching your dog his boundary limits, be
sure that he is solid in the Stay Command, and preferably
in the Halt Command as well.

B. One person can apply the teaching techniques of
boundary limits, but it helps if there are two people to keep
the dog from running away from you while you teach the
lesson – especially if your dog is fast and highly challenging.
By yourself you will have to be very quick to cover all the
area your dog could bolt to and cross the boundary.

C. In step F of training it's very important that you **do
not stop** when you give the Stay Command. Your verbal
and hand signal command should be given as you are quickly
walking towards the outside of the boundary line.

"Z." On the challenge, be certain that it is a challenge.
Remember the definition?

If you believe that throughout this book I led you to believe in the importance of keeping the leash LOOSE, DISCIPLINE, and THE LOVE factor throughout the training, it's because I meant for you to believe it. BELIEVE IT!

Happiness is... **A Better Canine**

NATHAN AND RIPPER

Having the right marriage with your dog means that even the
children should be able to "half-way" control him.

LESSON #206
A FINAL EXTREMELY IMPORTANT THOUGHT...
TO PONDER

As not all humans are alike, not all dogs are alike either, and as not all methods work on all humans, not all methods work on all dogs; and, as not all humans have the same capabilities, the same is true of dogs!

Could you, as a man, imagine that you could have been successfully married to every woman that you have ever met? Could you, as a woman, imagine that you could have been successfully married to every man that you have ever met? Yet, look at the way we humans end up "in marriage" with our dogs!

Take for example, Mrs. Carillo, an 83-year-old woman, living alone in Vista, California. Her children did her the "favor" of obtaining a "darling" little Doberman PUPPY, for "protection and companionship." Six months later...you can fill in the rest! They came to the school for training, and although we were able to immensely help them, could we here, ever expect a successful marriage?

Then there was 50-year-old Mrs. Bandini and her son, the only other person living in their home in National City, California. Her son brought home an "adorable" Bull Terrier PUPPY. A year later, the son joined the Navy and moved away. When Mrs. Bandini came to the school the first time, I could hardly believe my eyes, the way the dog torpedoed her into my office. During the first couple of lessons, especially when we tried to do shocking maneuvers on the dog, Mrs. Bandini on several occasions ended up sprawled on the ground. I have never "lost" a student, not even when I was working with the blind, but this is one time when I thought, for sure that I would! Could we ever expect a true successful marriage here?

Sam was a stout, hardheaded, 75 pound Boxer. A guide dog trainee that had been in training longer than most. Sam's obedience and guide work were excellent, he knew all of the routines forwards and backwards, but relying on him as a guide dog proved impossible!

The basic shocking maneuver that a trainer uses to teach a guide dog to stop at curbs is to trip over the curb when the dog fails to stop for it. The dog **must** stop, no matter how small the curb. We are never out to hurt the dog, but certainly we are never out to hurt ourselves either. On a couple of occasions, when Sam failed to stop for a curb, I casually tripped to shock him, but was I ever shocked when the instant that I tripped, away he went, dragging me down the street!

On another occasion, I was practicing obedience with about eight dogs in my crew—Sam was one of them. As I stood in front of them, down the line I would go, as I commanded, "Shadow, down!...Goood girl! Max, down!...Goood boy. Babe, down!...Goood girl! Sam, down! SAAAM, dowwwn!" But...to no avail! I proceeded to engage my leash on Sam, and as I firmly jerked downward, I commanded, "DOWWWN!" But, Sam...he was like the Rock of Gibraltar. He held his position! Again I jerked, and Sam...again **he held**! I proceeded to put my foot on the "U" section of the leash, which I was holding about 12 inches from the ground; my intention was to blast him down. With all my might I shoved my foot downward as I commanded, "DOWWWN!" In the process, I all but broke my leg, but Sam...**he held!** And as Sam held his position, he looked at me with beady eyes, lips quivering and curling upwards, a 1001 teeth showed as he lightly growled, as if to say, "You do that one more time, and for you it just might be...curtains!" With a blind person, Sam would never reach "the altar."

Take the following scenario and multiply it a 1000 x 1001 x 1000:

When we are **strolling, just passing by** the pet store
and we spot this "ever-so-cute" ball of fur and we fall madly
in love! Of these how many will be successful marriages;
how many will still be "in love" in six months to a year
later.

At the school for the training of guide dogs, we were
fortunate if 50% of the dogs that we obtained for training,
completed the training and actually became guide dogs. And
of those who became guide dogs, we went to extreme lengths
to match the temperament/personality of the dog with the
personality of the prospective blind master. In many instances, the match just wasn't there. But with others it was
like The Lone Ranger and Silver, Tarzan and Chita, and
Dorothy and Toto.

But... on the other hand, the match of the Lone Ranger
and Silver, Tarzan and Chita, or Dorothy and Toto did not
happen overnight. Much work and much patience had to
be endured.

Do you have the right marriage with your dog? Or
would both of you be happier if **the environment** was
changed? If you have too many obvious push-come-to-shove
type situations, perhaps you would be better off changing
the environment. This would possibly be kinder to both of
you. If you do have the right marriage, will you and your

dog ever become a Lone Ranger and Silver? Chances are that with persistence, patience, hard work and much love you will! But...if not...!

Take for example the story of yours truly and **MY RAMBO**. I first met Rambo at his home in El Cajon, California. A beautiful German Shepherd, weighing 100 pounds, standing 26" at the shoulder, 45" from nose to back; not including his tail which looked more like a python, and a head that resembled The Great Pumpkin! Rambo (not a name given to him by me) was **in need** of training. He had eaten the jacuzzi, destroyed all the landscaping, and he charged any door that was open. He was pushy and aggressive with all humans, and especially aggressive with other dogs. **He was a genuine hardhead.** Otherwise he was just a BIG TEDDY BEAR!

We began the training, but the owners quickly gave up. Rambo was just **"too much to handle!"** As I arrived one day for a lesson, the owner handed me a note which read, "To David Ruiz – a PRESENT! Because of his love for dogs, Rambo will spend the rest of his life with him..."

At the beginning, it was **very hard** to control Rambo. My two other dogs, Prince and Honey, had for years been used to being with me – Rambo wanted to eat both of them. One day, to control him (I thought) I left him in the

DIANA AND RAMBO

"...Otherwise a big TEDDY BEAR!"

bathroom at the office. When I returned about two hours later, Rambo had eaten the bathroom door, destroyed the window, torn out the telephone wires and all the carpeting. It looked like a tornado had passed through. A friend of mine once said, that in his previous life, Rambo must have been a bulldozer!

For the next several months, things didn't get much better. He ate the entire lining of the back of one of the station wagons, and on another he ate the back seat. I've had to stop many fights between him, Prince and other dogs. Once he even bit a little girl. And he has eaten more chicken bones than any other dog I've ever known. The trash can just seems irresistible to him. I can not even begin to tell you how many times he and I have gone 'round and 'round because of the trash. I have **never** made heavier corrections than the ones I made on Rambo! Mouse traps in the trash can. Forget it! He eats them too!

Today is Sunday, May 26th, and Rambo is 3-years-old. Last night I had chicken for dinner. I wrapped the bones in newspaper and put them in the refrigerator until I could dispose of them where Rambo could not get at them. I went to church this morning, 7:00 a.m. Mass. I left Rambo and Honey at home, and guess who got into the trash again while I was gone!

Three weeks ago when Rambo had a "trash attack," it was late at night, and I just wasn't up to making a scene of a correction. I took Rambo to the kitchen, opened the cupboard door under the sink, where I keep the trash, put his head in the trash can, closed the doors around his head, and with the leash secured them all – Rambo's head, trash can and doors! I left him there for about 45 minutes. On a couple of occasions, during this time, I passed by and exclaimed, "Oh, you like getting into the trash! Fine! Enjoy it!"

After the 45 minutes, I went back to him, untied the leash and before I let him go I struck the cupboard doors with my fist and as I did, **"This is a no, no, no, no!** Now you be a good puppy! **This is a no!"** I turned him loose, and away he went...to sulk.

Four days later Rambo got into the trash – AGAIN! I followed the same routine – 55 minutes this time. About a week passed. It was late, I was in the bedroom sitting on my bed. Rambo came in and nuzzled his big head under my arm and side. I put my arm around him and embraced him, and while doing so, Rambo was making a funny noise, like "smacking" his lips. "Smack, smack! Smack, smack!" I looked at him and exclaimed, "Rambo, did you get into the trash **again?"** I went to the kitchen. There was trash all over the place. This whole episode was so comical, or heartwarming

or...that I-just-didn't-have-the-heart-to-make-a-correction –
the way the big lummox came into the bedroom and nuzzled
me. It was almost like he was saying, "Gee, Dad, I did
it...again! I just couldn't help myself!" I picked up the trash
and put it away.

Will Rambo and I **ever** make a Lone Ranger and Silver?
I think so! With much patience, a few tears, maybe a little
more blood, (mine,) sweat and...**lots of love!**

Will **you** have a **solid** marriage **with your dog?** **I
think so!**

My best wishes and good luck to you!

May God bless you...**both**...and **your "marriage!"**

RICHARD, AIMEE AND RINGO

SUMMARY OF LESSONS

A. Don't miss out! Do not cheat yourself and your dog, read, chew, savor, and swallow this book **from cover to cover. Enjoy!**

B. Follow the lessons in the order given in the Table of Contents.

C. Keep practice sessions to 20 to 30 minutes. No more than three sessions per day.

D. If you have a practice session with your dog every day, one week between lessons should be adequate, otherwise two weeks is recommended.

E. Assure yourself of the dog's comprehension to the current lesson before advancing to a new one.

F. Keep the training environment conducive to learning.

G. Commit Lesson 101 – A Through Z Tid-Bits To Ponder And Remember! to memory.

H. Keep in mind the psychology of exactly how the dog learns:

 1. From the dog's eyes, the family is viewed as The Pack. The Pack must have a leader.

 2. To establish leadership, there must be discipline and love.

 3. Discipline must be firm, sharp, to the point and implemented so the dog **does not** see it coming.

 4. Passive love follows.

 5. The soaking-in period of time is the last part of all corrections.

 6. The bottom line is **SHOCKLOVE!**

I. The training collar is a **shock**—not a choke—collar. Be sure of its proper use.

J. The training leash is simply an extension of the shock collar.

K. The Heel Command is the first official lesson. The dog's front paws must always be in line or behind your heels.

L. In the Advanced Techniques – At Heel lesson, jerks are substituted with shocking maneuvers. **Caution is in order here.** The maneuvers are meant to shock **not to hurt**.

M. Remember the following points when teaching the Sit and Stay Command:

1. Do not waiver. **Do not show your insecurities!** Carry yourself, your commands and the various steps you take almost in a slow-motion manner. To the dog, this will make **you** appear confident and sure of your self. The dog's tendency will be to respond in kind.

2. Do not use the dog's name.

3. Do not lean over. Stand erect at all times.

4. Should the dog at any given time break position, **do not** go running back to him! Do not let him train you!

5. When teaching the Sit Command, **caution** must also be taken not to hurt the dog's lower back when you place him.

N. Before applying Lesson 107, Solving Misbehavior Situations, be sure that you have, in fact, gained your leadership over the dog through the application of Lessons 101 to 106. To attain maximum benefit, it's highly recommended that Lesson 107 be read more than just once.

O. The Down and Stay Command should be taught only through the natural submissiveness of the dog. Remember: Who is bigger? Who is the higher power? Who is the leader?

P. When teaching the Come Command, remember the nature of the dog's vision and requirement of movement.

1. Before you try the Come Command Off Leash, make sure that your dog **can with out hesitation**, respond to all basics commands, including the Come Command On Leash.

Q. Key points to be remembered when teaching the Unsupervised Stay Command are:

1. Bear in mind that the Unsupervised Stay Command is an advanced lesson. Before attempting to teach it, the dog should know that **you are the leader of the pack!**

2. When you show yourself to the dog, **you** must appear like gangbusters. You must get through to him that you are very upset!

R. The Go to Your Place Command – I encourage you to very definitely teach this command to your dog.

S. The Halt Command, Boundary Limits, and Automobile Riding Techniques are **essential** for your dog. Follow the various steps **explicitly** as given in the lesson plan.

T. Dog training is not an exact science, it is an art – the rules are not set in cement. **You** are the one on the firing line. **You** can and should make any adjustment you deem fair, necessary, and proper.

"Z." Don't miss out! Do not cheat yourself and your dog, read, chew, savor, and swallow this book **from cover to cover.** There is **"filet mignon"** to be had in each and every section. Enjoy!

OFF-LEASH CONTROL

" Dis ... is ... not ... da ... way!"

OFF-LEASH CONTROL

A question which is often asked by the students is, "How do I get to the point where I can control my dog Off Leash?" Based on experience, the answer is simple in theory but not so simple in application. It goes back to:

A. The beginning of training.

B. The follow through of **correct** methods during training.

"Z." The end results of training.

And in simple terms, the end result of training is, **who is the leader of the pack?** If you have:

A. Diligently worked with your dog at least 20 minutes every other day during the training period.

LELAND B. HOUSMAN, M.D. AND LEE

OFF-LEASH CONTROL

"Dis ... is ... da ... way!"

B. Kept the leash **loose** at all times after the Advanced Techniques at Heel lesson.

C. Corrected him **correctly,** when the dog needed it.

"**Z.**" And... showed him lots of love when he did perform, there is no reason why at the end of training there should be any doubt in the dog's mind as to who the leader is. If not, you will have to work a little harder and a little longer. But remember, that if the dog knows On Leash, there is no reason why he should not perform Off Leash. **Remember the definition of the challenge (see pages 110 and 265).** Make a few **swift** corrections and watch them work **magic** for you. **Practice does make perfect!**

On the other hand, do not be afraid to take a chance. Give the dog the benefit of the doubt. On graduation, when I have the students perform their routines, they are always surprised when I ask them to "drop the leash and perform without it." In better than 90% of the cases they're **amazed** that they were able to complete the routine **without holding onto the leash,** including the Come Command!

At the school for the blind, while practicing out on the streets (on the firing line), it was **seldom** that a blind student would hear me holler "HALT!" regarding an obstacle. **Some chances had to be taken!** In other words, before I halted a

NADINE AND SAMPSON
OFF-LEASH CONTROL

C. ...da way!

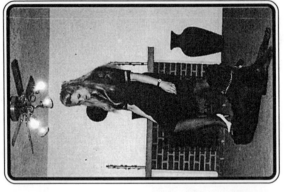

B. ...is...

A. Dis...

student and his dog on a potential dangerous obstacle, I let the dog have the benefit of the doubt and have him guide his blind master around it. Some were close encounters, however, the end result was blind masters and dogs who became expert travelers regarding any obstacle situation in a sighted world.

If you have been diligent in training your dog, give him the benefit of the doubt. **Take a chance, take the leash off,** and make your corrections as you go. I assure you that the majority of you will experience **miraculous results.**

To reinforce the basics of ending with a well trained dog, periodically, we drill the students with the following bottom-line questions. So that your dog will be well trained, you are urged to study the questions and their answers.

THE BOTTOM LINE

A. Instructor: Who is going to be the leader?

Student: All human members of the pack!

B. Instructor: How are we going to establish our leadership over the dog?

Student: We establish our leadership over the dog

through discipline, love, and the soaking-in time period!

C. Instructor: Explain what is the only **fair way** in which discipline should be issued?

Student: Discipline must be firm, sharp, to the point, and preferably where the dog **does not** see it coming!

D. Instructor: What about if the dog **does** see the discipline coming?

Student: If the dog does see the discipline coming, then it is no longer discipline, but aggression, and aggression **could** give rise to retaliation!

E. Instructor: What about the love factor?

Student: After discipline, one must come back with passive love! This is what creates a **"Good Bond"** between the human and the dog. Love should also be given every time the dog obeys a command or displays good social interactions.

F. Instructor: What is meant by the **soaking-in** period of time?

Student: The soaking-in period of time is the time which is given to the dog to settle and remember, or relate to the correction that transpired just beforehand.

G. Instructor: When issuing discipline, are we ever out to hurt the dog?

Student: When issuing discipline, we are **never** out to hurt the dog.

H. Instructor: What is the bottom line by which a dog learns?

Student: The bottom line by which a dog learns is SHOCKLOVE and LOVE.

"**Z.**" Instructor: And here we highlight **THE BASIC** relationship that we have with our dogs –

WHAT WE WOULD OR WOULD NOT DO WITH OR TO A HUMAN BEING...DO OR DO NOT DO WITH OR TO A DOG...PERIOD!

THE GRADUATE

B.J. Simone, "owner" of Joseph and Carol Simone

GRADUATION

For the majority of the students, graduation day is a very special day. Many of them bring their cameras and other goodies!

When I arrived at Carlos and Martha's home in Chula Vista, California, for the graduation of their dog, Cinco, we had a regular Mexican fiesta. Piñata and all! Many of the students have cake and ice cream. A Chinese couple in Poway, California, prepared the most elaborate and delicious Chinese dinner I have ever had.

On arrival at Bob and Veronica's graduation of their two Cairn Terriers, I was greeted with a glass of champagne; and no sooner was the first bottle gone when another one popped out! It was a great party! The evening got late and fuzzy, we had to reschedule graduation!

On graduation day, besides teaching the last maneuvers, the students are asked to perform what they and their dogs have accomplished during the training period. Before presentation of their Certificate of Completion we ask the students three questions. On completion of training your dog, we now ask you these same three questions:

A. In your mind, go back to day number one, when you first started working with your dog, and picture him as he was or as he would have been had you not trained him. Bring him to today and compare him as it relates to **obedience, behavior, and overall living with your dog at this time.** On a scale of 1 to 100%, what score would **you** give him?

B. In your mind, go back to day number one, and in this case, **look at yourself** as it relates to practice with your dog on the basis of a **daily routine, follow through of training methods on a moment to moment basis, and overall handling abilities.** On a scale of 1 to 100%, what score would you give yourself?

C. Same question as "B" as it applies to **all** family members?

Give your answers on the following page.

A. Dog's Name: _____

                        Score:_____%

B. Your Score:_____%

C. Family's Score:_____%

It has always been of interest to me that **no one** ever gives a score of 100% to their dog, the family or themselves. Now that **you** have completed training, as it relates to Dog vs. Humans, **who** do you suppose the majority of the students score the highest?

CONGRATULATIONS!

This is **your** book — **personalize** it; at the end you will find an easy to prepare certificate of completion.

BRING OUT THE GOODIES!
THE CELEBRATION CAN START!

I WISH I WAS THERE WITH YOU!
HAVE FUN!

GRADUATE GALLERY

CATHY AND KANANI

DAVID, CHARLES, AND SAM

DONAVAN, CHARGER, AND DAVID

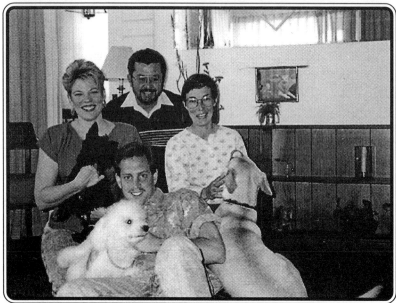

**ANN AND ABBEY, GREG AND FROSTY, CHRISTINE
AND DEMI, AND DAVID**

CHERI, DANIELLE
AND BERNIE

**DIANE, DREW
AND MILLIE**

**DOUG, PAULA
AND RIPPER**

DAVID, TONY, LINDA, AND TEQUILA

CONGRATULATIONS!
SALUD!

"AND THANK YOU, DAVID!"
"Hey, I want some too!"

"Save" yourself ... and your dog! Today's Dog World is a lucrative one. Beware! Do not be in a hurry to accept any new fandangled whatever! Pay the fair price for PROVEN modern discoveries, but not for useless paraphernalia — "miracle" training leashes, "miracle" training collars, "miracle" training methods, "miracle" pills! Stick with the time-tested, proven and successful.

The majority of dog problems ARE NOT dog problems, they are HUMAN problems. Therefore, the next time that YOU THINK you have a dog problem, turn to the pages of this book and don't just LOOK at yourself, but look and ... "SEE;" and if you "SEE" clearly enough, you will SEE the solution to your ... "dog" problem.

Dogs DO NOT NEED caviar and champagne, nor do they NEED to live as in a pent-house! Regarding any "new benefit" for dogs, simply apply ... THE KISS PRINCIPLE.

Happiness is... A Better Canine

"So...Prince, you may now take your bow for the people!"

POSTSCRIPT

At the end of the training talks and demonstrations, I would casually turn to Prince and suggest: "Prince, you can now take your bow!" Without fail, Prince would always curtsy for people – who would just love him even more! He was...THE BEST!

You can easily teach this trick to your dog. All dogs are notorious strechers after they have been sleeping or just lying down. So...each time you see your dog stretching, simply in a very friendly tone command, "BOWWW...GOOOOD DOG!" You will find that, in time, you have just to command, "BOWWW!" and he will give you...THE PERFORMANCE!

DAD AND I

"Oh, My Pappa...."

POST POSTSCRIPT

At special graduation ceremonies, when we are relaxed, many of the students ask about my background, my demeanor – the method to my madness!

I have all my life been very high on America and the American Way – America does not negotiate with terrorists; when the going gets tough, the tough get going.

The United States Marine Corps touched my life immensely. One of my many role models is President Abraham Lincoln. Dale Carnegie and his teachings are ingrained in me, as are lifelong influences from priests and nuns. The flavour of my foundation is spiritual fruit – but, religious nuts are not on my menu!

I consider myself a man of great fortune having been blessed into a wonderful large family with exemplary ole' fashioned principles and standards, and **ONE** wonderful, honest, strict, fair, and lovable leader of the pack – DAD!

The Author

Please SHARE the "good news," THE TRUTHS in this book with your friends and your loved ones — for it, I THANK YOU!

Better yet, why not just ORDER A COPY for them — they make a wonderful present!

ABC (A Better Canine) School For Dogs
7330 University Avenue
La Mesa, CA 91941-6003
www.abcdogtrainingtruths.com
(619) 466-1877

Happiness is... **A Better Canine!**

School for Dogs

This certifies that

through *text home study and training

have successfully completed

"The ABC's of Dog Training"

and the corresponding

"Dog Obedience and Behavior Course"

as outlined by this Organization.

In Witness Whereof, this Certificate is

issued under our hands and seal, in the

City of La Mesa, California

this   day of

Director

*The ABC's of Dog Training…and You!